Denver's Enduring Legacy

The Castle Marne

Fascinating stories as told by
Jim Peiker

ISBN-13: 978-1723583278

Design: David Robison

Dedication

I dedicate this book to...

*My mother who taught me to love without bounds and to believe;
my wife and best friend Diane who has shared my dreams, mothered
my children, and has made my life full of love and unquestioned faith;
my daughter Melissa without who this dream wouldn't be, and who,
with her husband Louie, gave me three remarkable grandchildren who
brighten my life; my son Riley who has shared the dream
and continues to fill my life with love;
my father from whom I have learned to have vision
to strive, and to share; and, finally, to my brother
Eddie and his wife Sue,
who have always stood by me.*

My love to you all,

Jim

Acknowledgments

My sincere thanks and appreciation to my family for
their love and support. Also, a very special thanks to our
dear friends Louise and Tom Teague, for recognizing
the importance of our project.

My thanks to Dr. Charles Brantigan for his wonderful biography of
William Lang, which I used to write my chapter on
Denver's most prominent historical architect.

We are very indebted to Chuck for his dedication to
our neighborhood through his Uptown Forum
and many efforts in Denver's historical
preservation community.

Likewise, special thanks to David (Brock) Brockway,
our general contractor, without whom our Castle Marne
might not have even been.

Preface

Write a book about my family and our Castle Marne experience?

I can honestly say that it had not occurred to me. However, looking back, the experience with the Castle has been extraordinary, to say the least. All together it is a story that cries out to be told. I must say that second to my marriage to Diane, and our 65 years together, buying the Castle is the most noteworthy event in my life. I have no regrets or feelings of remorse about the 29 years this building and I have spent together. The highs have been unforgettable, while the lows have, on the whole, been forgettable. Telling the stories has been the easiest and most enjoyable part. Putting all of the history, stories, and memories into a script format that makes sense has been the hardest and most challenging thing to do.

So many people have passed through our lives and have had significant effects on the development of our Castle Marne experience. When reading this book, you will find yourself inside Denver history and neighborhood history. You will meet the sequential owners and their families, and my family. You will sense our amazing connection when we first met the building.

Looking back, I can see how many times and ways the building had already touched my life before we met. Then you will understand the trials and tribulations of dealing with the city regulations, restoration, and renovation. Finally, you will meet our guests, oh my, our guests! We have had the most wonderful and interesting array of guests who have made everything so very worthwhile and memorable.

*"A good storyteller
is a person who has a good memory
and hopes other people haven't."*

Frank I. Cobb

Table of Contents

CHAPTER ONE

The Dream

Pioneers ✤ Prosperity ✤ Emerging City

Gold Rush

In the early summer of 1858 a small group of gold prospectors from Lawrence, Kansas arrived seeking gold and established Montana City on the banks of the South Platte River at Little Dry Creek. This was the first settlement in what would become the Denver Metropolitan Area. The site faded quickly due to poor findings by miners. Most of the settlers and some structures moved north to the confluence of the South Platte River and Cherry Creek. They staked a new settlement on the north bank of Cherry Creek and named it St. Charles.

In October, five weeks after the founding of St. Charles, the town of Auraria was founded by William Greeneberry Russell, a Cherokee Indian. The town, located on the south side of Cherry Creek, was named for the gold mining settlement of Auraria, Georgia. It was established in response to the high cost of land in St. Charles and gave away lots to anyone willing to build and live there. A post office was opened in Auraria in January, 1859, serving the 50 cabins that had been constructed. A short time later a third town, called Highland, was founded on the west side of the South Platte River. Surrounded by steep bluffs and separated from the other two settlements by the river, it was slow to develop.

In November 1858, General William Larimer, a land speculator from eastern Kansas, placed logs to stake a square-mile claim on the site of the St. Charles plat, across the creek from the existing mining settlement of Auraria. While the majority of the settlers in St. Charles had returned to Kansas for the winter, they left only a small number of people behind to guard their claim. Larimer and his followers gave the representatives whiskey, promises, and threats until the St. Charles claim was surrendered. The name of the site was changed to "Denver City" after Kansas Territorial Governor, James W. Denver, in an attempt to ensure that the city would become the county seat of Arapaho County, Kansas. Ironically, when Larimer named the city after Denver to curry favor with him, Denver had already resigned as governor and no longer had any influence in naming the town.

Word was out and the Pike's Peak or Bust Gold Rush was on. By the spring of 1859, tens of thousands of adventurers were coming across the plains for fame, fortune, and gold. Denver became a supply town when big gold strikes were discovered in the mountains to the west.

John Wyman

John H. Wyman of New York City arrived in Denver on August 1, 1866, via the H. O. M. & X Company Stagecoach, which took over five weeks to cross the plains. He registered at the Planters House Hotel and began to establish himself as one of the City's first "suburban" land speculators. The original U.S. property patent for the land that would become Wyman's Addition, belonged to Elias G. Mathew, who sold it to George H. Fryer for $200. Wyman bought the land from Fryer for the princely sum of $3,000 on December 8, 1866. John Wyman, as with speculators before and since, "banked his land." He sat on it through the 1870s. On three separate occasions in 1872, 1874, and 1875 he redeemed the property from tax sales at the eleventh hour. With the coming of the railroad in 1870, Denver grew from an 1860s supply town of 5,000 to 6,000 people into a thriving metropolis approaching 100,000 people by the 1880s.

Wyman's Addition was officially platted on August 30, 1882. In 1883, he donated a full city block at 16th Avenue, between Williams and High Streets, for an elementary school. The building was the most expensive schoolhouse the city had yet seen costing nearly $98,000. When the school opened in 1891, the neighbors gratefully named it Wyman Elementary School. He also donated one-half of a block from 16th to 17th Avenues, Race to Vine, for construction of the Denver Orphans' Home. In 1902, it was moved to a newer, larger location located at East Colfax and Albion Street. It is still there today.

Wyman set about developing the raw land into Denver's finest residential neighborhood. Detailed surveys were made, building sites platted, wide streets laid out, and sidewalks identified. Wyman's Addition would be Denver's first major subdivision featuring all city services including fresh water and sewerage, electrical and gas utilities, and served by the Colfax tramway line.

In 1887, he sold Wyman's Addition, comprising almost thirty-five blocks, to the real estate firm of Porter, Raymond and Company, for $300,000. The approximate boundaries were 17th Avenue on the north, Franklin to the west, York on the east, and 10th Avenue on the south. The firm of W.W. and I.B. Porter, with their partner Charles A. Raymond, ranked among Denver's most liberal and progressive real estate brokers. Charles Raymond made his fortune and built his mansion on the southeast corner of Colfax and Race Street in 1888. The home was later occupied by "Big Ed Chase," kingpin of Denver's gambling and sporting world. The home was torn down in 1925 to build Denver's penultimate 1920s movie house, the Aladdin Theatre, which opened October 27, 1926. The theatre was demolished in 1988 to make way for Walgreens Drug Store.

Wilbur Raymond - *First Owner of the Mansion*

Wilbur S. Raymond, who was the younger brother of Charles, came to Denver upon graduation from Wesleyan College in 1876. He worked in the mining and general merchandise business until he joined his brother's firm in the mid-1880s. The firm set about to market Wyman's Addition as Denver's premier neighborhood catering to the city's "Nuevo riche" society. Denver's premier architects were represented, from the Barrison Brothers, Balcomb and Rice, to William Lang, and Frederick Sterner.

Running through the middle of Wyman's Addition was said to be the finest, widest tree-lined residential avenue between St. Louis and San Francisco. If you struck it rich in the mines or in cattle ranching out on the prairie, you built your mansion along Colfax Avenue to flaunt your new wealth.

Wilbur Raymond, now a partner in the firm, would build his home on lots at 16th and Race Street. The Denver building permit shows he built the home for $40,000 on land purchased for $15,000. They selected William Lang, considered the finest eclectic architect in Denver, to build a mansion worthy of their dream. This would be the

"Show Home" and the model house for Wyman's Addition. Nothing was spared.

In 1887, Wilbur Raymond had purchased every lot on the east side of Race Street, all the way to Colfax. In 1890, after he built his house, he sold the remaining 10 lots to George Titcomb who contracted with William Lang to build five houses on speculation. Only two remain. The house next door, at 1560 Race Street, was built in 1894 by the Pullman Real Estate and Construction Company on lots that were originally the side yard of the Raymond House.

First owner, Wilbur S. Raymond and his family lived in the house for less than two years. He lost the house to creditors, but continued in the investment business in Denver until 1898.

In an article about the mansion on January 1, 1890, the Denver Republican noted, "The fact that men are able to build and maintain such houses and the further fact that they possess the taste for these elegant domestic surroundings, proves to the world that Denver has reached the social age in which refinement, culture and love of the beautiful stamp the character of the people."

CHAPTER TWO

The Affluence
Fortune ✣ Factory ✣ Family

James Platt - *Second Owner of the Mansion*

Colonel James H. Platt, three-term member of the U.S. House of Representatives; founder of the Equitable Assurance Co.; builder of Denver Paper Mills Co.; the Mansion's second owner.

Second owner, James H. Platt, was born in St. John's, Canada, on July 13, 1837. His family moved to Burlington, Vermont. He graduated from the medical department of the University of Vermont in Burlington in 1859. During the Civil War he entered the Union Army as first sergeant of the Third Regiment, Vermont Volunteer Infantry. He retired with the rank of Colonel. After the war, he settled in Petersburg, Virginia, April 1865. He served as member of the State constitutional convention in 1867, as well as member of the city council. Upon readmission of the State of Virginia to representation, Platt was elected as a Republican to the 41st, 42nd and 43rd Congresses. He served from 1870, to 1875. In 1870, he was secretary for the National Republican Congressional Executive Committee. During the 43rd Congress, he served as chairman of the Committee on Public Buildings and Grounds. He was an unsuccessful candidate for reelection in 1874. President Grant offered him the position of Surveyor General of Colorado, which he declined. In 1876 he moved to New York City, where he formed the New York Refining Company. He later sold it to John D. Rockefeller's Standard Oil Company.

Colonel Platt married his wife Sarah in 1884 and in 1887 they moved to Denver. He served as president of the Equitable Accident Insurance Company, as well as investing heavily in Denver real estate, especially in the City of South Denver, which was a dry, conservative suburb south of Alameda Avenue. In 1892, the Platts became proud owners and residents of 1572 Race Street. In June of 1894, Colonel Platt and

Sarah took a vacation at Green Lake, near Georgetown, Colorado. While fishing alone on the lake on June 13th, Colonel Platt fell into the water and drowned. He was fifty seven years old.

Later that year his widow Sarah sold the mansion to John T. Mason and his wife Frances.

"Paper Now King"

In 1890, Colonel Platt and Sarah developed plans for The Denver Paper Mills Company, which would become the finest paper mill in the country, if not the world. It was the largest business building complex in the state. Ground was broken September 20, 1890, with occupancy August 12, 1891, at a cost of $357,000. It advertised itself as the largest single mill for the manufacturing of paper in the United States. The mill was located along the South Platte River in the unincorporated City of Manchester Heights, along with the Platte Valley Cotton Mill and the Griffin Wheel Works, forming Denver's newest major industrial district. It was served by the Denver and South Park Railroad. Business was so good that in 1892 an additional mill was built just to the west, bringing their total investment to well over $500,000.

Denver citizens left Union Station in 13 Union Pacific Railroad cars to Manchester Heights to see the new factory and attend the grand opening celebration, held on August 23, 1891.

The *Rocky Mountain News* reported, "There were twelve to fifteen hundred persons attending. A few noticed promiscuously (sic) were Governor Routt, Mayor Platt Rogers, Charles Wheeler and Judge Owen LeFevre." That day's newspaper headlines shouted "Paper Now King."

During the ceremony several city and state politicians were present and gave speeches praising Denver's newest venture offering new opportunities for employment. Colonel Platt, in his speech to the crowd said, "There was a time when cotton was king. Advances and increased intelligence have dethroned cotton and paper takes its place. The human mind can hardly comprehend the vastness of the interests depending upon paper, or measure the calamity, which would over-whelm the human race if paper should cease to be produced. Next to Denver's great smelters, the successful establishment of cotton, iron, woolen, and paper mills are of the greatest importance to the rapid and permanent growth of our city. We have one of the largest and finest modern paper mills ever constructed in this or any other country."

The mill struggled for several years, mainly due to the latent results of the silver crash of 1893, finally going into receivership in 1899. In June 1900, Charles Robinson Smith of New York bought the bankrupt facility, paying off a debt of $50,457. The next year, United States District Court Judge Moses Hallett gained possession of the mill, reorganizing it as the Rocky Mountain Paper Company. Soon the name was changed to the Platte River Paper Mill. Several attempts were made to re-open the mill, but all were unsuccessful.

In 1910, Harry Tammen's Sells-Floto Circus wintered its circus and animals in the vacant mill. Around 1914, World War I chemical warfare material was manufactured in the mill. Ernest Braukman was the owner of the old paper mill at that time. In 1925, when he was General Manager of the Bankers Supply Company, he bought and moved another company, The Continental Label, Litho and Folding Paper Box Company, from downtown Denver into Colonel Platt's old paper mill. The name finally became Continental Paper Products Company.

Mr. Braukman committed suicide in 1932. Some said as a result of questionable financial affairs he encountered serving on the board of Colorado Women's College. His son Clarence took charge and ran the company until 1942.

On a personal note, my father served in France during World War I. Lying about his age, he joined the Marine Corps and was shipped to France. When he was found to be under age, he couldn't serve in battle. Instead, he served as a motorcycle courier taking messages from the front lines to General Pershing's command headquarters. After the war, he returned to Denver where he bought a horse and wagon and began a delivery business in downtown Denver. One of his customers was the Continental Label, Litho and Folding Paper Box Co., located in downtown Denver at 18th and Blake Street. After a few years, he was hired as a shipping clerk. There he met Helen Flo Sullivan, who worked as a stenographer. She had recently arrived in Denver from Pryor, Oklahoma. They began dating and were married in 1927.

I was told there is a wooden beam in the old warehouse section with "Ed ♥ Helen" carved in it. My father and his brothers, Albyn and Walter, worked and advanced in the business until they bought the company and the mill in 1942. Soon after, they sold the company to the Central Fiber Products Company of Quincy, Illinois, a subsidiary of the Carey Salt Company of Hutchinson, Kansas.

On September 9, 1956, a major fire damaged the center portion of the original mill. The company continued to operate the business in the undamaged portions of the building. A new factory was built to the south of the original mill. In March, 1964, the remaining sections of the original mill were demolished. The 155-feet high original smoke stack, the last remaining part of Colonel Platt's paper mill, was last to be demolished. Several construction cranes with huge wrecking balls began to pound away at the foundation of the stack, but it would not fall. Finally, the tallest crane had to begin demolition starting at the top, which finally brought the smokestack crashing down. It wasn't until the next day that the job was done. It was a fitting reminder of Colonel Platt's strength, resolve, and belief in his dream.

I was there to see it!

1930 picture of Continental Paper Products building, originally Colonel Platt's Denver Paper Mills Co.

CHAPTER THREE

The Disasters
Jewels ✦ Scandals ✦ Curse

Horace Tabor

Horace Austin Warner (H.A.W.) Tabor, Colorado millionaire, mine owner, Colorado Lieutenant Governor, U.S. Senator.

Horace Austin Warner Tabor, known as H.A.W. Tabor, was born November 26, 1830, in Holland, Vermont. He died in Denver, Colorado, on April 10th, 1899. Horace left home at age 19 to work in stone quarries in Massachusetts and Maine. In 1855, Horace joined one of the first groups organized by the New England Immigrant Aid Society to populate the Kansas territory with anti-slave settlers. He began farming land along Deep Creek, a tributary of the Kansas River, in what is today still called "Tabor Valley." His hard work and willingness to help the Anti-Slavery Cause also got him elected to serve in the "Free Soil" legislature, which sat in defiance of the so-called legitimate territorial government. This was an often-violent period of civil unrest that came to be called "Bleeding Kansas."

Early in 1857 Tabor returned to Maine in order to marry Augusta Pierce. They spent the next two years trying to make the farm productive, but succumbed to the stories of gold being discovered in the extreme western part of the Kansas Territory, now Colorado. They left Deep Creek in the spring of 1859 with their son Nathaniel Maxcy Tabor, who was not even two years old. They came to Denver via the Republican River trail. It took them six weeks of struggle across a barely explored landscape. It was "the acme of barrenness and desolation," according to Horace Greeley, who took the same route barely a month after the Tabors.

For the next twenty years the Tabors foraged for riches among the mining camps at Payne's Bar, Oro City 1, California Gulch, Buckskin

Joe, and Oro City 2, finally settling into Leadville. Typically, Augusta would board, bake for, and minister to, the miners, while H.A.W. tried his luck at placer sluicing or panning. Mostly, he was Augusta's partner in keeping the store and in running the post office and bank for the various camps. They were "sturdy merchants, beloved for their honesty and generosity." Tabor was known to be a generous man and it paid him big dividends. On April 15, 1878, Tabor opened his store as usual. Two German immigrants, August Rische and George Hook, walked in and asked Tabor if he would grubstake them with equipment. Tabor did; three times. The first cost him a mere $17.00. A month later, on May 15, the group knew they had a bonanza on their hands with the Little Pittsburg Mine. By the end of the summer they declared a $10,000 dividend to each. This was all that was needed to spark Tabor into quickly becoming the acknowledged leader of the silver mining community. He was later to buy, among others, the famous Matchless Mine.

The Tabors' good fortune didn't sit well with Augusta, whose chaste New England sensibilities were short-circuited by their suddenly unlimited wealth. She continued to behave frugally and dress modestly. She still took in boarders. She refused to "paint" her face as other women did. It might be said that the seeds of epic tragedy were sown in Augusta's too cautious reaction to overnight riches. For as much as she loved Horace, her view of what life should be like when one is middle-aged and fabulously rich, diverged irreconcilably from his by the close of the heady 1870s.

Baby Doe Tabor

In 1880, an attractive 25 year-old young lady named Elizabeth Bonduel McCourt Doe, a recent divorcee, arrived in Leadville. She was admired by Horace Tabor, and he soon began a discreet relationship with her. By July of 1880 however, it was no longer a secret. Horace moved out of his home with Augusta and asked her for a divorce. She refused.

Horace then secretly secured a divorce in Durango, Colorado. But it was not legal. Whether Horace knew this and was simply defiant, or whether he truly didn't know is unknown. But the fact remains that he and Elizabeth, to be forever known as "Baby Doe," were secretly married in St. Louis September 30, 1882.

When Augusta Tabor learned of the St. Louis marriage, it was too late to contest it. Horace continued to defend the divorce relentlessly. Augusta fought equally as vigorously. She asked for separate maintenance, claiming her husband was worth over $9 million. Tabor denied it, which was probably true. More accurate estimates put his worth at about $3 million.

The scandal of the alleged divorce and marriage raged on, and was Front-Page news across the country. It was an embarrassment to Washington, as well as prominent figures in high social circles.

On March 1, 1883 the marriage between Horace and "Baby Doe" was finally legalized. Augusta Tabor eventually received a good part of the Tabor fortune said to include $10,000 per month in a final divorce decree. She moved to Pasadena, California where she died a wealthy woman, February 1, 1895. Many say it was from a broken heart.

Elizabeth Bonduel McCourt "Baby Doe" Tabor, second wife of millionaire Horace Tabor. She wore the "Isabella Jewels."

The Jewels

Horace Tabor's fame grew, he even served briefly as a U.S. Senator. Through political favors, he was able to secure a 30-day appointment to Henry Teller's vacated senatorial position. He was sworn in as Colorado's Junior Senator on February 3, 1883; married on March 1, 1883. He bragged he would marry Baby Doe in Washington D.C. at the new Willard Hotel, with President Chester Arthur, his staff and Cabinet in attendance, and he did! Their wives refused to attend the scandalous affair. For a wedding gift, he gave Baby Doe a set of jewels purported to be the jewels that Queen Isabella of Spain pawned to send Christopher Columbus to the new world.

> "When Horace was near death, Mrs. H.A.W. (Baby Doe) Tabor gave her brother, James M. Court, her diamonds then worth $18,000 to deposit in the bank. Upon the death of Horace on April 10th, they were seized by his creditors." (*The Denver Times*, April 28, 1899)

> "Among the collection of diamonds, which are supposed to be the finest ever owned by a lady in this state is the celebrated diamond, the 'Queen Isabella.' The history of the stone reads like a page from a fairy tale. The stone dates back to 1462, and was one of the original jewels pledged by Queen Isabella of Spain to furnish money for the equipping of a fleet for Christopher Columbus when he started on his voyage of discovery to America. The wonderful jewel has been in possession of most of the crowned heads of Europe and the story is related that it was in possession of Mary, Queen of Scots, when in the gray dawn of February 8th, 1587, she was beheaded at England's Fotheringhay Castle. After knocking around European capitols it made its way to America." (*The Denver Times*, May 9, 1899)

Silver Crash

The Sherman Silver Purchase Act was a United States federal law enacted on July 14, 1890.

It increased the amount of silver the government was required to purchase on a recurrent monthly basis to 4.5 million ounces. The Sherman Silver Purchase Act had been passed in response to the growing complaints of farmers' and miners' interests. Farmers had immense debts that could not be paid off due to deflation caused by overproduction, and they urged the government to pass the Sherman Silver

Purchase Act in order to boost the economy and cause inflation, allowing them to pay their debts with cheaper dollars. Mining companies, meanwhile, had extracted vast quantities of silver from western mines; the resulting oversupply drove down the price of their product, often to below the point at which the silver could be profitably extracted. They hoped to enlist the government to increase the demand for silver.

Under the Act, the federal government purchased millions of ounces of silver with issues of paper currency. In addition to the $2 million to $4 million that had been required by the Bland–Allison Act of 1878, the U.S. government was now required to purchase an additional 4.5 million ounces of silver bullion every month. The law required the Treasury to buy the silver with a special issue of Treasury (Coin) Notes that could be redeemed for either silver or gold. Gresham's law then took over. The artificially overvalued currency (silver) drove the artificially undervalued currency (gold) out of circulation. In the metals markets, silver was worth less than the government's legal exchange rate for silver vs. gold. So, investors bought silver, exchanged it at the Treasury for gold dollars, and then sold these gold dollars in the metals market for more than they had paid for the silver. They took the profits on this transaction and bought more silver. They did this over and over. This would continue until the Treasury ran out of gold. After the Panic of 1893 broke, President Grover Cleveland oversaw the repeal of the act to prevent the depletion of the government's gold reserves.

The Silver Crash of 1893 was a devastating blow to the entire nation, but was especially damaging to the silver producing western states. It was the worst economic panic until the Depression of the 1930s.

Riches to Rags

When Congress repealed the Sherman Silver Purchase Act in 1893, the government was no longer in the market for silver. Prices dropped lower than the operating costs needed for the silver mines, and it became impossible to continue operations. Horace Tabor, failing to listen to the advice of others to diversify, faced ruin. In the interim, and adding to the crisis, Tabor had also made a number of unsuccessful, if not unwise, investments in foreign mining ventures that failed. He lost huge amounts of money in Mexico and South America. His reserves was gone, he and "Baby Doe" lost everything. But regardless of the now destitute condition of the Tabors, Horace never lost faith in the future, and until his dying day he always found work of some kind, hoping to recapture his lost wealth.

At age 65 he was shoveling slag from Cripple Creek mines at $3.00 per day until he was finally appointed Postmaster of Denver just a year before his death. Before Horace died he was said to have told Baby Doe, "Hang on to the Matchless Mine, if I die, Baby; it will make millions again when silver comes back." On the morning of April 10, 1899, in a small room at the Windsor Hotel, Horace Tabor died of appendicitis.

For the final three decades of her life, Baby Doe, the once best-dressed woman in the West, lived in a shack on the site of the Matchless Mine enduring great poverty, solitude, and repentance. After a snowstorm in March 7, 1935, she was found frozen in her cabin, at about 81 years old. During her lifetime she became the subject of malicious gossip and scandal, defied Victorian gender values, and gained a reputation as one of the most beautiful, flamboyant, and alluring women in the mining West.

My father remembered seeing her walking up 17th Street from Union Station dressed in men's work clothes and a slouch hat with her feet wrapped in burlap bags.

The Ballad of Baby Doe is an opera by the American composer Douglas Moore. It is Moore's most famous opera and one of few American operas to be in the Standard Repertory. The opera premiered in the Central City Opera House in 1956, and returns every 10 years.

Tabor Gems to go on the Block

"Famous Diamonds Owned by Late Senator to be sold at Auction to Satisfy Loan. Diamonds, including the famous Isabella jewel, deposited by Mrs. H.A.W. Tabor, second wife of the late senator, with the Continental Trust Company to secure a loan of $8,650, and said to be valued at $25,000, will be sold at public auction at the front door of the trust company on December 16.

It is said that N.M. Tabor, an adopted son of the late senator, will be present, and that in all probability he will be the purchaser.

Officials of the trust company refused to discuss the sale last night, but admitted that, the sale would take place on this date, and that Tabor had signified his intention of being present and bidding on the diamonds. Mrs. Tabor had placed the diamonds with the trust company more than a year ago and secured a loan on them, but it is said that her note has become overdue and that she is unable to redeem them, and hence the decision of the trust company to sell them at public auction. While the sale has been announced as a public auction, yet it is understood that the diamonds will simply be put up for sale, and that N. M. Tabor will name an amount he will give for them and they will be turned over to him.

The diamonds, which are valued at between $20.000 and $40,000, according to different estimates, while not numerous, are rare. They were purchased by the late Senator H.A.W. Tabor for his second wife, and were held by her until reverses came upon the aged millionaire and he was forced to mortgage them to Herman Powell to secure a loan." (*Rocky Mountain News*, December 7, 1907)

Who Would Save the Tabor Jewels From Auction?

"Unless friends of Mrs. H.A.W. Tabor, widow of the late senator, succeed in raising $8,000, the collection of diamonds which were given to the Continental Trust company in security for a loan of that amount one year ago, will be sold at public auction today.

A subscription fund was circulated Saturday to raise the amount, and something more than $2,000 was obtained. It is hoped to raise the remainder before the sale takes place today to prevent the collection going under the auctioneer's hammer. The diamonds are valued at considerably more than the sum for which they were pledged, and the friends of Mrs. Tabor are planning to pay off the loan and sell the jewels singly to much better advantage. In this manner she will be able to reimburse the subscribers and also obtain a good surplus." (*Rocky Mountain News,* December 16, 1907)

John Mason - *Third Owner of the Mansion*

"TABOR DIAMONDS SOLD AT AUCTION TO REPAY LOAN $25,000 to $45,000 Worth of Gems Pass Under the Hammer for $8,750. One of the Diamonds, Isabella Pawned to Help Columbus knocked off to the highest bidder for cash. The Tabor diamonds of historic fame and variously valued at from $25,000 to $50,000 were sold this morning before the entrance to the Continental Trust company's bank to John T. Mason, 1572 Race Street, for $8,750.

The jewels had been deposited by Mrs. H.A.W. Tabor, second wife of the late Senator Tabor, with the Continental Trust company to secure a loan of $8,650, and was thought that N.M. (Maxcy) Tabor, son of the senator would bid them in. John W. Springer was the auctioneer, and about a dozen persons were on hand to bid, among them A.L. Abrams, one of the vice presidents of the Continental Trust Company's bank. Only three bids were received, the first a bid of $8,000, and the second a bid of $8,500, when Mr. Mason bid $250 more, and the stones were turned over to him." (*Denver Post*, December 16, 1907)

Diamond Ring

Quoting from an article in The *Rocky Mountain News*, dated March 30, 1935, about Baby Doe shortly after her death, a missing ring from the Isabella collection is mentioned.

"Edgar C. McMechen, administrator of her estate, turned his attention to learning what has become of the famous blue white stone, valued at more than $6,000. Historians know Baby Doe loved that diamond, not for its intrinsic worth, but for its sentimental memories.

Fate of the valuable gem has remained a mystery since January, 1905. John Springer, a Denver banker, returned it to the tearful Baby Doe, after it had been advertised for sale. The stone had been put up as collateral, along with a number of the Isabella jewels for a loan of $17,500 to satisfy the note when Mrs. Tabor and Silver Dollar (her daughter) appealed to Springer.

All the jewels were sold or given to Denver residents with the exception of the ring, which Mr. Springer gave back to Baby Doe. She told him she treasured it and would never let it go the way of her other jewels."

Urban Legend

John Mason bought the Isabella Jewels in 1907. John Mason's first wife Frances often wore the jewels to Denver's high society affairs. She died in 1911. His second wife, Dora Porter was given the jewels at her wedding to John Mason in 1912, and we are told she wore the Isabella Diamond.

The diamond ring was not in the inventory of William Barth, who purchased the jewels from John Mason's estate in 1914. Could this be the gem that urban legend says is still hidden here in the Castle Marne?

William Barth

Nothing was known about the collection, until a May 29, 1914 Denver Post article appeared with the headline:

"BARTH HELD IN SPELL OF 'BAD LUCK' JEWEL. The Isabella Diamond, sold by the Queen of Spain so that Columbus might find New World, brought woe to the widow of Horace Tabor. Millionaire William Barth took possession of the jewels including the Isabella diamond on the death of Herman Powell. Not long after, both his wife and son died."

Mrs. Fitz-Brind

"J. Fritz Brind is again pursued by the evil of the famous Tabor Diamond. The third wife of reputed millionaire files suit for divorce charging repeated acts of cruelty, beginning soon after wedding. Divorce was granted". (*Denver Post*, January 28, 1921)

"The collection of diamonds belonging to the first Mrs. J. Fitz-Brind, who died in November, 1914, is valued at $19,700 according to an appraisal of the stones by expert Denver jewelers. She obtained the jewels from William Barth. Included in the collection is the famous Tabor diamond, set in platinum, once reputed worth $75,000, which has been appraised at $1,500. The disposition of these jewels has not yet been made. Before Mrs. Brind was operated upon in August of 1914, she delivered her diamonds to the International Trust company, with a document disposing of them among friends and relatives.

The company was to deliver them to those named in case she died as a result of the operation and to return them to her if she recovered. Mrs. Brind lived for two months after the operation, but never took the jewels from the trust box.

The beneficiaries are now trying to get the jewels, contending that the operation was the indirect cause of her death. Her husband claims that the jewels belong to him since Mrs. Brind did not immediately die after the operation. A lengthy court battle ensued." (*Denver Post*, December 3, 1915)

CHAPTER FOUR

The Benefactors
Museum ✤ Children's Home ✤ Park

John Mason

John T. Mason, the Mansion's third owner, philanthropist, famous lepidopterist and a founder of the Denver Museum of Nature and Science

John Thomas Mason, the third owner of the Mansion, was born in Lincolnshire, England in 1853. In 1872, at the age of 19, he immigrated to New York. Soon after that, with his brother, he moved to Mississippi, then to Galveston where he accepted a clerical position in the wholesale dry goods establishment of P.J. Willis and Bro. After a year, he resigned this position, opening a small mercantile venture on his own account. He moved his business to Houston in 1880, occupying the building at the SW corner of Main and Prairie. His business prospered to such an extent that larger quarters were required. In 1886, he purchased the Phoenix Building. In 1887, after a complete renovation, he opened The Mason Dry Goods Arcade, and a year later, the six-story Mason business block. Through wise investments, he acquired a considerable fortune.

In 1892, he retired at age 40, selling his business interests to his nephew. Over two years were then spent traveling Mexico and Central America collecting specimens of moths and butterflies adding to his renowned collection. In 1895, opting for a higher and drier climate, John Mason and his wife Frances moved to Denver, where they purchased the mansion from Colonel Platt's widow Sarah, paying $40,000.

LIFE OF THE BUTTERFLY, LIVING BLOSSOMS PASSING AN EPHEMERAL EXISTENCE

"Denver can boast of a resident whose fame as a butterfly chaser is worldwide.

One of the best collections of butterflies in this country, or any other country, is the property of Mr. John T. Mason. He has one of the best collections of 'marble whites' in this country, of which there are seventeen varieties.

Mr. Mason was born in Lincolnshire, England, and as a boy displayed the instincts of the born naturalist. He had when he was 15, a very fine collection of birds, birds' eggs, and butterflies. In 1877 he was married to Miss Frances Schaffter of Galveston and they had made their home in the south until the charms of the Italian climate of Colorado brought them further north and west. Their home at 1572 Race Street was bought last August but not occupied until November. It is their intention to make this their permanent home."

(*The Rocky Mountain News*, May 17, 1896)

Another claim to fame for John Mason was that he purchased the Queen Isabella Jewels in 1907, when Horace Tabor's estate was sold at auction to satisfy a loan.

In 1912, fifty-nine year-old Mason, a widower, married thirty-seven year-old Dora Porter. His first wife Frances had died in 1911. Dora was the eldest daughter of Henry Porter, whom Mason had a relationship with through the Denver Museum venture. As a wedding present to his bride, John presented her with the famed Isabella jewels. Following the wedding the couple settled into Denver society and got involved in several social and civic issues in the city. Well respected for their efforts and generosity, the Mason name would later be included in the list of Denver's pioneer benefactors inscribed on the marble wall of the Greek Amphitheater in Denver's Civic Center Park.

John and Dora began to "winter" at their Pasadena estate beginning in 1913, permanently moving there in 1918, at which time he gave a portion of his famous moth and butterfly collection to the Denver Museum of Natural Sciences. There are at least 20,000 varieties of butterflies in Mr. Mason's collection and counting his duplicates he must have more than twice that many of these beauties and fragile denizens of the air. A long-time collector of butter-flies and moths, Mason's collection of many thousands of specimens, soon caught the attention of enthusiasts across the country.

The idea for a museum of natural history in Denver was first proposed by Breckenridge pioneer, Edwin Carter in 1892. By 1899, the city of Denver accepted Carter's proposal. His entire collection of stuffed birds and animals, displayed in Breckenridge for many years, was the nucleus of the proposed museum, founded on December 6, 1900. Henry M. Porter, an early pioneer and wealthy Denver business-man, was one of the first Denver citizens to back what would become the Denver Museum of Natural Science. Others followed, including John T. Mason and John F. Campion. Mason donated portions of his moth and butterfly collection and Campion donated his impressive collection of gold specimens from mines in the Breckenridge area. Mason was the superintendent of construction, and when the new museum finally opened in 1908, Mason became the first curator and business manager.

BUTTERFLY COLLECTION GIVEN TO CITY MUSEUM HAS RARE SPECIMENS John T. Mason - Will Present to Denver Results of Lifetime of Work, Study and Investigation Extending Around the World

"Butterflies, green, gold and iridescent, and measuring six inches from tip to tip: butterflies demure and brown and less than an inch across: butterflies that look like velvet and those that look like jewels—thousands and thousands of the winged creatures may be soon be seen in Denver. The City Park museum has been enriched by the gift of Jack T. Mason's collection of moths and butterflies, one of the finest in the United States."

(*The Rocky Mountain News,* July 28, 1918)

One of the rarest American butterflies in Mr. Mason's collection is the hipparchia pgalla, which comes from Arizona. Probably there is not an entomologist of any note in the world who is not acquainted by reputation, with the magnificent collection of Mr. Mason, and like Katisha's Elbow, (a mountain place in Alaska), "hundreds of people go miles to see it." It is at once the envy and the despair of the collector.

JOHN T. MASON IS DEAD IN CALIFORNIA

"John T. Mason, capitalist, art connoisseur and sportsman died at his home in Pasadena, Calif., Thursday, according to a telegram received by Denver relatives from his widow, Mrs. Dora Porter Mason. Retiring from business, Mr. Mason devoted himself to a study of nature, to hunting and fishing, gathering a world-famous collections of butterflies and fostering the arts-especially music." (*The Denver Post*, December 7, 1928)

After his death, the remainder of the Mason Collection was given to the museum by Dora Porter Mason and went on exhibit from 1929 to 1938, when they were temporarily withdrawn to design a more contemporary exhibit. It is interesting to note that all of the collection was not to be seen by the people of Denver until 1940. The exhibit closed in 1986, when the wing in which it was housed was demolished to make way for museum expansion (IMAX Theater).

Lepidopterists from around the world come to the museum to study Mr. Mason's collection. Because of the historical significance of the Mason Collection, specimens remain in storage and are available for study. All of this is a fitting tribute to "Uncle Jack," as he was known. John Thomas Mason is buried in Houston, Texas, in Glenwood Cemetery beside his first wife, Frances Schaffter Mason.

Mason and the Denver Orphans' Home

The Ladies Relief Society formed Denver Orphans' Home in 1876 in order to take care of the orphans being brought in to build railroads and work in the mines of Colorado. In 1881, Margaret Evans, wife of former territorial Governor John Evans, realized that Colorado needed a facility for the thousands of poorly-housed or homeless children. This realization led Evans to open the Denver Orphans' Home (renamed the Denver Children's Home in 1962). With the help of Iliff, Warren, the wives of Charles Berger, Walter Cheesman, William Clayton, Charles Kountze, David Moffat, Chester Morey, Fred Solomon, John Routt and other women, the Denver Orphans Home would become a reality.

As John Wyman was preparing his pending application for annexation of his subdivision into Denver, he donated land for Wyman Elementary School at 16th and Williams, and land for the Denver Orphans' Home at 16th to 17th on Race Street. In 1883, the first residence was built. It was a three-story building on a half-block site at 1600 Race Street. Within days, 40 children filled the Denver Orphans' Home. By 1889, several hundred children considered Denver Orphans' Home their home. The facility included a barn, chicken coop, and a small hospital.

By the turn of the century, the neighborhood had become one of Denver's most desirable.

I can imagine John Mason, along with his business partner Henry Porter (one day to become his father-in-law), sitting in the Dining Room of his elegant mansion looking across the street at the orphans' home and musing how the neighborhood would certainly be more desirable without the orphans' home.

It seems that "interested" parties approached the Denver Orphans' Home and offered to aid in the relocation of the orphanage to a location further east, with larger, newer quarters and land to expand. In 1902, the home moved to its current location at 1501 Albion Street. It is a 50-room complex, designed by prominent Denver architects Willis A. Marean and Albert J. Norton. The building's exterior looks much the same as the day it was built in 1902. Now known as the Denver Children's Home, the organization still provides youth services to the community. But the unfortunate history of this 138-year-old organization includes numerous exorcisms, a fire that claimed the lives of several children, and the spirit of a sullen, lonely bride who wanders the halls.

The block across the street of 1572 Race was redeveloped, beginning with the home at 1600 Race Street, built in 1904 for Armistead L. Abraham. He was a prominent citizen of Denver, vice president of Continental Trust, and an agent for American Bonding Company of Baltimore. He later became president of Althoff Manufacturing Company. Armistead L. Abraham was present at the auction when John Mason purchased the Queen Isabella Jewels in 1907.

In 1912, the home at 1600 Race Street was sold to Edwin Morrison, whose family was associated with Proctor and Gamble. He would become a vice president of the Great Western Sugar Company. As senior executive, he was in charge of design and construction of sugar refineries throughout the west. He died at the age of 89, followed by his wife Florence in 1961. The mansion was converted into a nursing home, the E & E Guest House.

In 1966 the building was given to the Colorado Tuberculosis Association, later to become the Colorado Chapter of the American Lung Association. The carriage house was rented to the League of

Women Voters. In 2005, it became part of the Argus Home Health Care company.

The Denver Orphans' Home, directly across from the Castle, 1881-1901.

Dora Porter Mason - *Houston's Mason Park*

Wife of the Mansion's third owner, John Mason. Responsible for Houston's Mason Park; Trustee and supporter of the Denver Museum of Natural History.

"The 70 acre tract of heavily wooded land in the East End was presented to the city by Mrs. Dora Porter Mason of Denver, in memory of her late husband, John Thomas Mason, prominent pioneer Houston businessman. The gift was accepted formally by Mayor Walter E. Monteith and council, at a special session Saturday morning. Paul R. Timpson, President of the Houston Land and Trust Company and a longtime friend of the Mason family, presented deeds to the city in behalf of the donor. Combined with 34-acres of city owned land, the gift tract will make a recreational center of more than 100 acres. Brays bayou, which takes a winding course

24

through the park, will offer splendid boating facilities, officials said." (*Houston Post-Dispatch*, November 30, 1930)

"In 1930 Mrs. John T. Mason gave Mason Park to the city in memory of her husband, Houston businessman. A few months ago she made an additional gift of $15,000 with which to build equipment for the park. The result is its model lighted recreation center. Sixty six flood lights turn night into day for the benefit of those who wish to play tennis, basketball, softball and other games or spend an evening picnicking or just sitting and resting.

Mrs. Mason has come to Houston from California where she now lives, and will dedicate her gift Tuesday night. Her late husband came to Houston from Galveston in 1880. He prospered in the mercantile business and had faith in Houston so he invested his surplus in real estate. In 1890 he was able to retire from business and in 1892 he built the Mason Building on Main Street. This was the cornerstone of his fortune and it enabled him to live a quiet and leisurely life until his death in 1928. The park that bears his name is a fine memorial to him and a magnificent gift to Houston which will keep his memory always as green as the pines which rustle above the playground."

(*Houston Press*, May 25, 1936)

In 1939, in her late husband's name, Dora gave funds to construct one of the finest municipal swimming pools in the country in Mason Park. This is an excerpt from a letter she received from the Houston Land and Trust Company, July 6, 1939.

"Dear Mrs. Mason, the swimming pool in Mason Park has been recently completed and is now in use. I don't know of any park in Houston that is better located, better equipped and more universally patronized than the John T. Mason Park. Our people will always feel grateful to you for your liberal contributions to their pleasure and happiness."

"Thousands of Boys and Girls Learn to Swim in City Pools without charge."

(*The Houston Post*, July 9, 1939)

Dora died in 1940. She left $25,000 in her will to the City of Houston for Mason Park improvements.

Henry Porter along with his daughter Dora Porter Mason, contributed $1 million and a substantial portion of land for the building of what today stands as Denver's Porter Memorial Hospital. Along with her sister Ruth, she was very involved in the founding and development of the Denver Botanic Gardens.

CHAPTER FIVE

The Evolution

Changing Face ✣ Changing Times ✣ Changing History

Adele Van Cise - *Fourth Owner of the Mansion*

Adele Van Cise, fourth owner of the Mansion.

In 1918, following John Mason's move to California for health reasons, Adele Van Cise purchased his property. Adele Van Cise was married to Edwin Van Cise, a practicing attorney in Deadwood, South Dakota in the 1870s and 1880s. Following the Wounded Knee Indian Massacres, he served as one of the prosecuting attorneys during those famous/infamous trials. In 1900, the Van Cise family moved to Denver with their son Philip and daughter Ethel.

Edwin Van Cise became a prominent attorney and First Chairman of the Denver Public Utilities Commission, as well as leading the Philosophical Society of Denver. For many years he was a lecturer in the law for the University of Colorado. He died in 1914.

As years had passed, our Capitol Hill neighborhood began to change. Rich folks who originally moved here and built their mansions and raised their families here, began to move further east up to the 17th Avenue Parkway, Park Hill, and the Denver Country Club areas. Colfax was becoming more commercial and the surrounding neighborhoods slowly changed into the mixed-use configuration we know today.

Adele set about converting the mansion into a seven-unit apartment house. There were two units on the first floor, two units on the second floor and three units on the third floor, which had been the Ballroom. All had private baths and kitchens. Adele lived on the first floor. The

Dining Room was her Parlor and the archway gave access to the original kitchen. A room was built on the back of the house as the new kitchen. Major construction made the Conservatory we know today.

Naming of Castle Marne

We were told that when Adele's son Philip saw the building his mother was turning into an apartment house, he remarked that it reminded him of castles and country homes he had seen along the Marne River when he served in France during World War I. Adele needed a name for her apartment house and decided to call it the Marne Apartments. Adele lived here until her death in 1938. It looked like a castle to our family, so we renamed it the Castle Marne.

Lyle Holland - *Fifth Owner of the Mansion*

In 1939 Adele's daughter Ethel sold the building to Lyle and Gladys Holland.

Lyle lived here until his death in 1972. His apartment was on the first floor south side. He was associated with Gus's Wholesale Bakery "No Muss No Fuss Just Leave It to Gus." It was located on South Platte River Drive off Evans, next to Overland Park Golf Course and across the river from Colonel Platt's old Paper Mill. Lyle Holland also conducted a small real estate management company from the Marne. He was married three times. His first wife Gladys subsequently came back and cared for him in his last days. He was an avid gun collector with a shop in the Carriage House where he loaded his own ammunition. We were told he only rented to single women, as they were less trouble. He let the neighborhood know that he roamed the property at night with a loaded rifle.

One day during our construction, a young woman came to our door and announced herself as Lyle Holland's granddaughter, Diane. She wanted to see what we were doing to Grandpa Lyle's house. I showed her around and she told me about his three-legged dog and confirmed the 'Ripley's Believe It Or Not' famous "upside down tree" story. She

28

asked if she could bring her Grandmother Gladys to see the house. We setup an appointment the next Sunday afternoon. We enjoyed Gladys stories about the neighborhood back in the 1940s and what it was like to operate a seven-room apartment house back then.

A few weeks later, I got a call from Diane Holland asking if she could bring her grandmother and several other family members back the next Sunday afternoon. She told me that Gladys had a gift for us. When they arrived they were carrying four large cardboard boxes. We opened the boxes to find the four sections of the Carrara marble stand you now see in our Foyer.

Gladys told us that when they bought the house in 1938 from Ethel Van Cise, Ethel asked her and Lyle if they wanted the plant stand, as no one else in Ethel's family did. Ethel said her mother told her it was a wedding gift from her husband Edwin, but she didn't want it and would sell it to Gladys and Lyle for ten dollars. After Lyle died, Gladys took the plant stand home with her. After the tour, Gladys told us the family had a meeting and they all agreed the plant stand should be back in the house. Of course we accepted their gift.

I recently came across a copy of a Christmas card from Lyle. We can see only the inside of the card.

"Wishing you and yours a Merry Christmas, and a 1970 New Year as fine as you wish it to be." Lyle Holland

On the left side of the card it is typewritten

"The Marne was completed in 1890 using Castle Rock, Colorado stone. Two-thirds of the butterfly exhiit in City Park was once in the building. It was a private home until 1918 when Adele Van Cise made it into seven private bath apartments. At the rear is a 28-foot by 40-feet garage with a five-room apartment above. At the alley is a 4-car garage made of brick. The three-and-one half lots are pretty well covered. The Hollands have owned it since 1939 and love and cherish the 'Castle.' Come and visit me at apartment zero."

Lyle Holland

Lyle died soon after, asleep in his bed.

Richard and Louise Dice - *Sixth Owner of the Mansion*

Richard was working for the 1st National Bank in Downtown Denver. He and Louise were living in an apartment on Gaylord Street. One summer evening in 1974, while on a bike ride, they first noticed a "big vacant old stone house with the beautiful window," on the corner of 16th and Race Street.

Richard told me Louise looked at it and said, "It looks like the project of a lifetime and it's for sale."

They bought it from Lyle Holland's estate, in 1975, for $130,000. Then the Dices got together with two young architect/carpenters named Paul Huffman and Brooks Bond, who set about to restore and renovate the Carriage House into rentable office space. It took over eight months to complete the project. The Dices then legally separated the property, established it with its own legal description and sold it apart from the main building. Richard told me they then had enough money to restore and renovate the main building. They first restored the third floor into an apartment, which they moved into, while reclaiming the basement, first, and second floors.

They originally envisioned a three-unit condominium, one on each floor, which after further consideration was not felt to be the best use of the property, as the nature of the neighborhood had begun to decline. They settled on a business property instead. In a small article about the house being renovated, *The Rocky Mountain News,* dated January 11, 1976, said "It has endured care varying from weepy-eyed love to flinty entrepreneurial stewardship."

Unfortunately, in 1978 Denver's economy suffered, as did the rest of the country. The Dices were not able to attract the businesses they had hoped for. They sold the property in 1979 and moved to Taos, New Mexico where Louise died on April 24, 2010.

Parolees

From 1979 through 1981 the building was leased to the State for a Federal program called the "Colorado Pilot Project on Rehabilitation of Paroled Criminals" or "Employ X." This experimental program was a processing center for paroled convicts from State penal institutions. They would be tested, interviewed, evaluated, and counseled. They didn't live in the house. However, they did leave rude notes and unpleasant graffiti around, reminding us of their time spent here. The funding for Employ X was pulled after an unsuccessful two-year trial. After that, an off-the-wall woman's magazine and an anarchist newspaper were among some business offices that were located here. Several attempts were made to further develop the property but its condition and the nature of the neighborhood precluded success. In 1981, a doctor bought the property. He wanted to turn it into a medical clinic.

Interestingly, Dr. Jules Amer, a prominent Jewish pediatrician, had just located right across the alley. Sadly, the doctor couldn't provide the necessary parking spaces for his proposed clinic and he walked away.

In 1985, the law firm of Feuer, Flossic and Rich became owners of the property. It was from them that we purchased the Marne in 1988.

CHAPTER SIX

The Legacy
Landmarks ✤ Legends ✤ Ladies

William Lang - *Castle Marne Architect*

William Lang, Castle designer and Denver's most prolific architect.

It has been said the life of William Lang would make an excellent movie. Hollywood loves a character that has seen such triumph and devastation in such a short life. William A. Lang was born in 1846 in Chillicothe, Ohio, the oldest of ten children in a family that moved often, just ahead of the law.

During the Civil War, Lang served in the Second Illinois Light Artillery. After the war he returned to his family in Illinois where he took up farming. The family moved constantly, ending up in Albion, Nebraska, where Lang married Delia Prisbey on December 20, 1877. Their only child, Mable Gertrude was born there in 1882. He soon established a prosperous grocery business. Lang began his career as an architect in Nebraska after selling his grocery business to his partner in 1884.

There is no documentation to show that Lang received any formal training in architecture. Much of what he picked up was probably through observation and widely available pattern books. After designing one of his two commercial buildings and a school in 1884, Lang became restless and moved his family to Denver in mid-to-late 1885. He was already listed as an architect and building superintendent in the 1886 Denver City Directory. Lang burst onto the Denver building scene at the peak of economic activity with a fast and furious pace. He designed over 250 buildings in his brief nine-year career in Denver, including three churches, townhouses, barns, a commercial building (A.M. Ghost Building), and numerous residential dwellings. He was known as Denver's residential architect. Perhaps most well-known are the Molly Brown House (1890) and Castle Marne (1890), which show Lang's preference for rusticated stone, turrets, arches, and the grandness of the Richardsonian Romanesque style and scale. His recognizable eclectic style was used not only on these large imposing mansions but also on townhouses (a few of which remain) and what he termed "moderate cost housing." Although he left Illinois before Richardsonian architecture made its mark, it is apparent that this style had a great impact on him and that he tailored it to his taste. It is difficult to pin Lang down to a definite style, for he merged many elements from different styles to suit his taste, not following convention. Lang designed most of his buildings in the early 1890s and was severely impacted by the Panic of 1893. It effectively ended his career as an architect and sent him on a downward spiral from which he would never recover.

His wife Delia left him in 1895, moving to Chicago. He sold his opulent townhouse and all of his possessions in 1895 before being admitted to St. Luke's Hospital in 1896. Lang was diagnosed with "softening of the brain." Today we call it dementia. In March, 1897, he was discharged to his brother's care in Englewood, Illinois. He disappeared from his brother's house on August 7th, wandering as far as Morris, Illinois, where he was arrested as a tramp and vagrant. He was so filthy that the jailer would not allow him in the jail and he was escorted to the edge of town and told not to come back. At 6:30 a.m. on August 24, 1897, while walking east from Marseilles, Illinois, he was hit by a train and killed instantly. While Lang had a brief but productive career in Denver, he left a legacy in his eclectic buildings that reveal the prosperity of Denver's early years. I find it truly amazing that Mr. Lang could accomplish so much in just a little over nine years.

He was buried at Riverside Cemetery, Marseilles, Illinois, in a Grand Army of the Republic plot with a regulation Union Army headstone.

Clarence Watkins - *Castle Marne*
Stained Glass Artisan

Since 1761, stained glass has been a Watkins family tradition. The history begins in England where family members made stained glass windows in London and Liverpool. Eight generations of Watkins men have devoted their lives to stained glass. Four generations of Watkins men have devoted their lives to stained glass and beautifying the Rocky Mountain area since the arrival of Clarence Watkins in 1868.

Clarence traveled to America with his toolbox in hand and skills he had learned from his forefathers, working in New York and Boston. In 1868, he left St. Joseph, Missouri, in a covered wagon loaded with stained glass, supplies and tools, destined for Denver, Colorado. He soon set up shop and as Denver began to grow, his traditional old-world style of stained glass became very popular in the mansions, businesses, and grand churches of Denver.

His son, Frank, followed Clarence in the art. Frank began his apprenticeship in Denver in 1902. He rode the stained glass glory days until the depression and during these lean years he would repair stained glass windows at no cost. His son, Phillip Watkins, was also taught the trade and helped his father until stained glass was interrupted during World War II due to the unavailability of lead. Philip Sr. served as a fighter pilot during the war and while in England, befriended the Liverpool Records Clerk and learned more about the Watkins family's stained glass ancestry going back to the 1600s. After the war he worked for thirty-five years during Denver's growth boom with his son, Phil, Jr. at his side.

Phil Jr. is the latest member to carry on the Watkins Stained Glass tradition. He has been in the studio since he was old enough to walk and made his first set of church windows unaided at age 12. He completed an official five-year stained glass apprenticeship, learning every aspect of the trade from the very basic skills to the most intricate painting and has been accepted into the British Master Glass Painter's Guild the British Society of Master Glass Painters. (I looked it up on the Internet.) Phil is one of the few artists in the country who can do every aspect of stained glass and during the past 50 years has fabricated many thousands of new stained glass windows. As a specialist in stained glass restoration, Phil was offered a position in England to work in English Cathedrals for the rest of his life, but declined, preferring to continue the Colorado family legacy.

Sarah Platt Decker - *Wife of the Mansion's Second Owner*

Colonel Platt's widow, Sarah Platt, was an incredible woman in her own right. She was born in Vermont in 1855 and reared in Holyoke,

Massachusetts. She was known for her motto, "Never groan, never sigh, and always keep step." She was a descendant of the Adams political family. As a teen, she was named trustee of a fund for the poor. In 1893, the Suffrage Bill made Colorado the second state to enfranchise women as voters. She was a leader in Colorado's women's suffrage achievements. She focused her attention on the welfare of women and children, becoming the first woman appointed to the Colorado Civil Service Commission and established the Denver Home for Dependent Children. She became the first woman to serve on the Colorado Board of Charities and Corrections and was credited for prison reforms. She established Denver's first Day Nursery, free seed distribution for neighborhood garden plots, and worked for the establishment of Mesa Verde as a national park. In 1894, she founded the Women's Club of Denver and was named its first president. She became national president of the Federation of Associated Women's Clubs in 1904. In her four years as president, she gave hundreds of speeches persuading members to take up the cause of women's suffrage.

Her husband, James H. Platt, died in 1894. In 1899, she married Westbrooke Decker, a prominent Denver lawyer and judge. Rumors had it that she wanted to run for mayor of Denver. She was Colorado's delegate to Theodore Roosevelt's Governor's Conference for the Conservation of National Resources, held at the White House in May, 1908. In 1910 Woodrow Wilson consulted Sarah in Washington D. C. concerning child labor. At the 1912 convention of the General Federation of Women's Clubs in San Francisco, it was widely rumored she was going to announce her candidacy for the US Senate. She died suddenly of kidney disease. She was 56 years old.

An obituary in a Denver newspaper described her as "Colorado's foremost woman citizen and the real leader of the suffrage movement in the United States." Another wrote that she deserved "a great share of the credit that Colorado became the first state in the Union to realize the political rights of women."

Her funeral eulogy reads, "Sarah Platt Decker was one of the most definite, courageous, imposing characters of the day and country. This daughter of sturdy, fighting Americans brought breeziness, optimism, and a vision to her new environment that set her apart in a community of colorful individuals."

The State of Colorado placed her body in the rotunda of the new Capitol building, "Lying in State," becoming the first woman so honored. The city closed its offices at noon the day of her funeral and ordered flags to fly at half-staff. Three Colorado governors were among the pallbearers. She was recognized again in 1913, when the new South Denver branch of the Denver Public Library was named for her. It was located in Platt Park, named for her husband Colonel James Platt. The Sarah Platt Decker Branch Library, built with Andrew Carnegie funds, is a charming Elizabethan structure of tapestry brick and a moss green tile roof reminiscent of Ann Hathaway's Shakespearean Cottage. Sarah Platt Decker was inducted into the Colorado Women's Hall of Fame in 1990. She was honored with a plaque at the League of Women Voters' headquarters in Washington D.C. as Colorado's "First Woman Citizen."

I attended McKinley Elementary School just two blocks north of Platt Park. As our school didn't have a library or auditorium, we spent a great deal of time at the Sarah Platt Decker Library.

Sarah Platt Decker, leader of Colorado's women's suffrage movement and vocal advocate for women's rights in the 1890s.

Philip Van Cise - *Son of the Mansion's Fourth Owner*

Philip Van Cise, son of Adele Van Cise. He drove the mob and the Klan from Denver.

Philip Van Cise took advantage of a split in Denver's Republican Party to win the office of district attorney in 1920; he was 36 years old. He ran under the campaign slogan, "A fighting Man for a Fighting Job." This referred to his five years of service in the Colorado National Guard, including six months spent on strike duty in the southern Colorado coal fields and his service in France during World War I, as a Lieutenant Colonel on the General Staff of the American Expeditionary Forces. He remained in the Officer Reserve as a Lt. Colonel until 1942.

A few days after winning the September primary, Van Cise was contacted by a former Denver Police inspector, who said he wanted him to meet a friend who could help him win the general election. At first he wasn't interested, but finally agreed to meet this contact, who turned out to be none other than Lou Blonger, boss of the Denver mob. After a few minutes of general conversation about local politics and how much a campaign cost, Blonger asked Van Cise if he was well-financed for the general election campaign. Van Cise was a bit taken back and replied that he had a little money, hopefully enough to see him through. "I've paid my own way so far and I don't think it will cost more than two thousand dollars," he said.

Blonger replied, "Two thousand dollars! It'll cost twenty five if it costs a cent. It's the most expensive campaign save the mayor's. Now look here, I'm serious about this. I like your style and I want to help you. I'll put up twenty five thousand; you can have it now, or call me as you need it."

Van Cise, who already knew a little of Blonger's life of crime, was astounded, but kept a straight face and replied, "I can't tell you how much I appreciate that offer Mr. Blonger. This is the first time I ever ran for office and I don't know much about the game. I don't need your money now. I want to get through without any outside help. But if I need it and it costs as much as you say it does, I will certainly call upon you. I don't know how to thank you."

Van Cise handily won the election without Blonger's money. A few days before he took office, Van Cise called Blonger and asked him if he could come to his office. He said to Blonger, "I know you are running crooked gambling joints and I am going to close them down." Blonger denied everything. After controlling Denver's organized crime for over 20 years, he left quite unable to believe what Van Cise told him. Was it just an idle threat? He didn't know.

The gang was well connected with politicians at all levels, but they would have no control over Van Cise, who was not beholden to the political power structure. At the same time, Van Cise received little backing in his effort from either the mayor, Dewey C. Bailey, or law enforcement officials, many of whom, it would later be shown, were in league with the con men.

Lou Blonger was an evil genius who dominated power in Denver's underworld. He was a short, heavy set affable fellow of French-Canadian descent, who came to this country from Canada in his early teens. He settled in the western mining camps in the early 1880s, working in gambling halls and saloons with his brother Sam, who was ten years older. They settled in Denver in 1880, operating a saloon and gambling hall with "ladies" available. As Denver became more respectable, they found themselves moving into elaborate bunco confidence game schemes. Robert Redford's movie, "the Sting," was inspired by the crime that flourished in Denver at that time.

By the turn of the century the brothers had so much influence in Denver that bunco gangs did not operate there unless under the Blongers' control and not without paying a hefty percentage to the brothers for every score. In its prime, the operation raked in as much as a million dollars a year. Blonger's influence at city hall, police head-quarters, the sheriff's department, and even the Denver Post and the U.S. Marshal's office, kept him out of jail and out of the spotlight on most all occasions. His control of the Denver bunco trade lasted over twenty-five years during which time none of the gang served hard time.

Lou Blonger became the most powerful and wealthy "fixer" in town with a private telephone line that ran directly from his office to the Chief of Police. His 60-man confidence ring in Denver and his multi-million dollar racket had branches in Florida, Havana, and California. He was the undisputed king of the Denver underworld.

Lou Blonger kept a pretty young mistress. Together they were seen often in Denver's high society. In 1921, he built her a beautiful bungalow on Capitol Hill in the 800 block of Williams Street, right across the alley from the fashionable Ascension Episcopal Church.

After Philip Van Cise became Denver District Attorney in 1921, (without Blonger's help) and as he learned more of the sordid details and extent of the Blonger gang's power, he set up an independent investigation of them, secretly funded by a group of wealthy Denver citizens and employing a handful of former federal agents and others he could trust. In 1922, Van Cise used a special force of Colorado Rangers to capture 33 suspects in a single day. Fearing that Denver Police or Sheriff's officers would tip off the gang once the first suspect was taken to jail, Van Cise detained the captured gang members in the basement nursery of the First Universalist Church, where he was a member, until the sweep was complete. In Colorado's longest and most expensive trial until that time, 20 con men, including Lou Blonger, were convicted and sent to prison, effectively busting the "Million-Dollar Bunco Ring." Blonger died in the Colorado penitentiary in Canon City, CO at age 73.

Van Cise also waged battle against the Klu Klux Klan during his four-year term in office. The Klan wasn't effectively driven from power until the late 1920s. Van Cise's life had been threatened, crosses were burned in his yard, and one attempt was made to kidnap him. He refused the call of many citizens to run for mayor to replace Bailey in 1923 and returned to private practice in 1925. Van Cise formed a law partnership with his former assistant district attorney, Kenneth Robinson. In 1936, he wrote and published his memoir of the gang-busting saga, *Fighting the Underworld*, which became an influential book in criminology circles.

Drama followed Van Cise into private life. For more than 20 years he served as an attorney for the *Rocky Mountain News*. During this time he aggressively defended the paper when sued for libel by Fred Bonfils, publisher of *The Denver Post*. Bonfils died before the case was tried.

In 1943, two men tried to kidnap Van Cise from his front yard. Then in 1945, the husband of a woman Van Cise represented in a divorce, marched into his law office and fired two shots at him. Fortunately, both missed. Philip Van Cise retired from practice in 1967 and died in Denver's St. Luke's Hospital on December 8, 1969, after a month-long illness.

Dame Beryl Windsor - *The Castle's Queen Victoria*

"Castle Marne owner Jim Peiker again celebrates Queen Victoria's Birthday with impersonator Dame Beryl Windsor at Afternoon High Tea." *Denver Post* May 23, 1999

Dame Beryl began portraying Victoria at the queen's birthday celebration every year at Castle Marne Bed and Breakfast. I built a riser that fit in the Turret in the Front Parlor, I also built a "throne" for her to sit on and greet our Tea guests.

She also performed at the Grant-Humphreys mansion and at various charity events at Saint John's Cathedral. She presently lives in Asheville, North Carolina, and occasionally is still doing her Queen Victoria performance.

In 1985 she was invested as a Dame of the Sovereign Hospitaller Order of St. John Jerusalem Knights of Malta. Dame Beryl Windsor is resplendent in black, the very image of Queen Victoria, who mourned her beloved Prince Albert for four decades. Her only concession to color was a little white lace on her sleeves and neck and the white veil. Otherwise, it was "40 years of black," said Dame Windsor, who has portrayed Queen Victoria at various events since 1995.

Her daughter sent pictures from the Victoria and Albert Museum in London, where she served an internship so that she could help her mother represent Queen Victoria as realistically as possible. Beryl went to the Bata Shoe Museum, in Toronto to see what shoes the queen wore. She found they were black silk decorated on the front with glass beads. She also has identified the type of earrings the queen wore. Windsor says, "I study before every performance. I re-create her language. She always addressed her subjects as 'My dear, dear people.'"

Though she speaks with a distinctly English accent, Windsor, no relation to the current royal family that I know of, was born in Houston while her parents were visiting the United States. Her father was involved in oil exploration.

They moved back to England when she was one-year old. Beryl was 10 years old in 1940 when her parents were determined to put her and her little brother, Allen, on a ship for America to escape World War II. Her father was in the British Air Force, stationed at Glascow, Scotland.

Beryl recalls living near the shipyards. The Germans bombed the yards almost every night. The family would go down into the basement to be safe, often standing in knee-deep water. She and her brother finally got a train to Liverpool to board a ship to the United States. The train was strafed by German fighters and many were killed, but she and her brother were not injured.

Their ship had a military escort for the first three days, but then they were set off alone sailing across the North Atlantic to America. Their ship was torpedoed by three German U-Boats and suffered damage. "I stood on the deck in a life jacket with two parakeet cages and holding my brother's hand ready to get into life boats. The captain told us to sing 'There Will Always Be an England' to keep our minds off the danger. Soon after he came round to say that he thought the best chance they had was trying to limp it to America," she recalled.

Days later the ship docked in Montreal. Beryl and her brother were taken in by a family for 10 days. She learned later that their mother and father had been notified the ship had sunk and that they were dead. After two weeks, arrangements were made to send them to Texas to be cared for by friends. Shortly thereafter, her brother was enrolled in a military prep school in Dallas, while she went to Atlanta and was schooled at the Washington Seminary for Young Ladies, now the West-minster School.

A lady who had graduated from the school heard about Beryl. She came every Sunday to tutor her in history and how to be a lady. It turned out it was Margaret Mitchell, the author. She took Beryl under her wing for three years. After lessons were over, they would talk about *Gone With the Wind*.

"Ms Mitchell told me she went riding every day with her father and an uncle, who would discuss the Civil War. They would point out houses and tell the story behind them, and that's what gave her the idea for *Gone With the Wind*." Beryl remembers.

After the war, Beryl returned to England aboard a troop ship. When she was 18, a friend took her to a political rally where she met Winston Churchill, who was very interested in her story and they spent over an hour together. She came back to the United States in 1952 and for three years did public relations for Radio Free Europe in New York City. Secretly she was recruited by the Polish Underground to care for an agent being held secretly in a New York Hotel. On another occasion, a distinguished man came to her desk saying it was urgent that he had to speak to her boss. She said he was in a very important conference. The man told her his name was Michael Hollenphaller. He was insistent. She recognized his name; he was the King Of Romania. During her years at Radio Free Europe, Beryl interviewed many German Death Camp survivors, as well as Eleanor Roosevelt.

She eventually moved to Denver, married a man who later died of injuries suffered from being tortured in a North Korean prison. She spent 25 years in the Denver office of the Federal Communications Commission investigating complaints. Windsor was on the board of Dr. Watson's Neglected Patients, the local chapter of the Baker Street Irregulars, a Sherlock Holmes admiration society. In 1995, the board president asked her to do a seminar and suggested something relating to Queen Victoria.

During most of her appearances as Queen Victoria, Beryl lectures on the Queen and takes questions. Victoria, the daughter of the Duke of Kent, fourth son of George III, and a German princess, was the longest-reigning monarch in British history, ruling the British Empire for 64 years. She married her first cousin, Prince Albert, in 1840. She fell in love immediately and it turned out to be a very happy marriage, which is unusual in royalty. She proposed to him, which is a proper thing for a queen. It was a great love match after they got to know each other.

He was 5 feet 7-inches tall, she was only 4 feet 11-inches. She wrote in her diary, "He's so beautiful."

Albert died of typhoid at age 41. Queen Victoria wore black for the rest of her life. She died in 1901.

"Queen Victoria set a wonderful example of family life," Windsor said. "No one who was divorced could come into the court. She was a steadfast person. She helped keep the Empire together. Her servants loved her. She had a great sense of humor, which was not always seen, because she looked so stiff in pictures. She was a fan of Sherlock Holmes. She wrote to the police during the Jack the Ripper murders suggesting they follow Holmes' detective methods."

God Save The Queen!

Dame Beryl Windsor portraying Queen Victoria with Diane and Jim by her side.

PART TWO

The Restoration

CHAPTER SEVEN

The Purchase

Ghosts ✤ *Determination* ✤ *U.S. Congresswoman*

Our Story Begins

My daughter Melissa and I were standing in the unemployment line, we were, as some say, between positions. I had been on the road as a manufacturer's rep, selling garage doors, electric openers, and a lot of other stuff. She had been working in the hotel field in both Denver and Colorado Springs. My wife Diane was teaching school at St. Mary's Academy and Louie, (Melissa's husband), was in New York working in the emerging computer technology business. Our son Riley was in college. We had casually talked of a family business and had explored franchise business opportunities, but nothing seemed to fit. A friend asked if we had ever thought about operating a bed and breakfast. We said no we had not, but maybe it would be worth looking into. Our friend told us there was a B&B for sale over in Capitol Hill on the corner of 16th and Race Street.

Well, we made an appointment to see the building. The day was January 22, 1988. The Victoria Oaks B&B on the southwest corner was a delightful property. Owned by two gentlemen from Albuquerque who had to return home because of family problems, and they were trying to sell it. There were seven rather small rooms, most with shared baths, and no food service preparation facilities. It was clean, well-decorated, and furnished catering to a gay clientele. It just didn't seem to be what we were looking for.

It was a cold, gray overcast afternoon. After looking at the B&B, we were standing on the front porch, when I looked directly across the street. For the first time I saw this three-story stone mansion, obviously vacant and in dreadful condition. It was an amazing sight! Being a Denver native I am certain I drove down these streets hundreds of times, but I never saw that building before.

We walked across the street and up the front steps. The building and yard were worse than you could imagine. There was a large sign in the front window showing a snarling dog and the words "KEEP OUT ATTACK DOGS WILL KILL." As we stood back gazing up at the amazing stonework, we saw bats circling the roof. We looked around a bit more and agreed that this building wasn't our bed & breakfast dream house. For the next month or so we looked all over Denver for a suitable location for our B&B. Either the zoning was wrong, or we didn't like the neighborhood, or it cost too much, or it was too big or too small. We began to wonder again about the "big old stone house on the corner with the beautiful window." I called the realtor and we got an appointment to see the interior. It looked worse from the inside than looking through the windows. It was cold and bleak and rather scary. Strangely, as we looked around it began to seem a bit less cold, bleak, and scary. We came back several times after that. Each time we seemed to feel that maybe it could be what we were looking for. But it still seemed an impossible job to turn this disaster into our dream.

The last time we visited the house, I noticed a business card lying on the Foyer fireplace mantel that I had not seen before. I glanced at it and put it in my pocket. We were still unable to imagine what it would take and wondered how and if it could be done at all. A couple of days later, I found the business card in my coat pocket. It read, "Kittredge Construction Company, David Brockway owner." I thought, *What the hell!* I called and told him how I came upon his card. He said that a few years ago he got the contract to restore and renovate the old Kittredge Building downtown on the 16th Street Mall and that's how he named the company. He knew the realtor with the listing on the old mansion. On a whim he called and asked if he could come out to the house and see it. On another whim, he left his business card on the mantel. The more we talked, the more I felt he understood our concerns and what we wanted to accomplish. Oh, and the Kittredge Building is built of rhyolite, a pale, fine-grained volcanic rock of granite composition. I said I would get back to him.

A Mutual Choice

Our family talked and talked and talked. Slowly we began to realize that we were really not trying to decide if that old building was for us, because strangely, we began to understand the house had decided we were for it!

Purchase Financing

The "big old stone building on the corner with the beautiful window," The Raymond House, a.k.a. The Marne, had been on the market for quite a few years. The asking price was down to $215,000. We didn't think they had had any serious offers.

We prepared a business plan, got our limited finances together and set out calling on banks for money to buy that big old house. Denver's economy was starting to crumble, as the Savings and Loan scandals were coming to light and Denver's Silverado Savings and Loan was right in the middle of it. Banks and S&Ls were not interested in talking to us.

On to Plan B!

Before my father died, he had deeded his Evergreen home to my brother and me. He had moved to Denver to be closer to medical services. Neither my brother nor I wanted to move to Evergreen, so it sat empty for several years. It was a delightfully comfortable home in the middle of 30 acres of beautiful mountain property about 4 miles south of Evergreen, Colorado. It was furnished with my mother's collections of Navajo Indian pots, rugs and baskets, as well as antiques and furnishings from our family home in Denver. After a flood and disastrous fire, the Evergreen home was a total loss. The property was valued at $160,000. I asked my brother if he would buy my 50% share. Bless him, he agreed; and, then with selling some stock and such, we came up with about $125,000. I called the real estate agent and told him we were ready to put in a bid. Closing was tentatively set for August 1st, Colorado Day.

We didn't know where the rest of the money was going to come from, but we were moving ahead. A friend of Louie, my son-in-law, said he knew of a man who had been a well-connected Denver banker, now in real estate with Grubb and Ellis. He was getting ready to move to Seattle because of Denver's economy. We called him and convinced him to at least listen to us. His name was Jim Lampman. He said he couldn't make any guarantees, but he would listen to us. Diane and I met him, explained our situation and asked if he would please help us raise the money we needed. Then when he saw the building, met with all of us, and heard our plans, I guess he kind of fell under the spell. He was able to obtain a bridge loan at three-points over prime, to cover the remaining balance to purchase the castle. The abatement of the asbestos remained a sticking point. We were able to negotiate a deal that if we paid for the asbestos removal before closing, the price would be lowered to $184,500. The asbestos was removed and we closed and took title on August 1, 1988.

We were now the proud owners of the "big old stone house on the corner with the beautiful window."

It was an up-hill battle, but now it's ours. 1988.

Another Mansion

A couple of weeks after we put in our bid, I got a call from a man who said he wanted to meet me because he had heard that we were trying to buy the old Raymond House. I asked him what this was about and he said he had information about the house that he wanted to share. We agreed to meet the upcoming Sunday afternoon at the house. When we met, he gave me his business card and introduced himself as Ralph Heronoma, the owner of Langstone Realty. The logo on the card was a drawing of the door and window entrance on the 16th Avenue side of our house. He named his company after William Lang, the architect of the house. He went on to say that he and his partner, Jim Alleman, had tried to buy the house two years before, but after many disagreements about water damage, asbestos abatement, deferred maintenance, and a list of other complaints, their earnest money was returned. They walked away from the deal. We started talking about the house and its owners and history. I began to sense that he had much the same feelings about the house that we did and that he wanted to be sure that I knew how much he cared about the "big old stone house on the corner with the beautiful window." I learned later from his grandmother that he was devastated when he couldn't have the house. She explained to me that as a boy he dreamed about owning and living in a mansion. He believed this was the one. She told him that this was not the mansion for him. It was meant for the Peikers and he would have his mansion soon enough. She told him, "Get over it, quit sulking, and move on."

Yes, they did get their mansion two years later.

The house, originally across the street from Molly Brown's House at 13th and Pennsylvania Street, was a grand single family home built during the 1890s boom years, for the Milheim family, early Denver pioneers. Eventually, it was turned into a rooming house, then converted to commercial office space, then slated to be demolished for 22 parking spaces. Instead, Ralph Heronoma and Jim Alleman took title and it became the largest structure to be moved in a single piece in Colorado's history. After the move to 1515 Race Street in September 1989, Jim and Ralph converted it back to a single family residence. They lived in and maintained office space in their dream home for 20 years. When Jim died, the house just didn't make sense anymore; it was so large. It was difficult for Ralph to leave, but he knew it was time. Now he finds it hard to go back because of all the memories.

I have to tell just a quick story about the Sunday afternoon when Jim's and Ralph's mansion had been towed up Colfax, around the corner to be lowered on its new foundation at 1515 Race Street. A gentleman approached Ralph, identified himself as an inspector for the Denver Building Department, and said that the building could not be set on its new foundation. He said the cement had not cured sufficiently. The building was up on wheels, sitting in the middle of Race Street. Somewhat flustered, Ralph asked him what would he suggest he do? The inspector almost casually said that Ralph should go down to City Hall Monday morning and take out a parking permit for his house. Two weeks later the house was set on the foundation. The rest of the story of Ralph, Jim, and the Milheim House is a book by itself. For the last five years it has served as home to the Lighthouse Writers Workshop of Denver.

Renovation Financing

Ron Abo Architects began drawings and blueprints for our Bed & Breakfast, now The Castle Marne. Kittredge Construction began assembling our restoration and renovation work plan. I began preparing our involvement with Denver's Landmark Preservation Commission and the National Historic Building Register. Filing for the 20% Federal Investment Tax Credit was an important part in our plans. I spent hours at the Denver Public Library and the Colorado Historical Society doing research on the history and owners of the building. Of course at the same time we worked up a new business plan and current financial information. I began calling on banks again, still without any success. After a couple of months of making appointments, proposals and explanations, and being told no, a Vice President of Century Bank North, named David Alley, said "maybe." If we could manage to get a partial Small Business Administration loan guarantee, they would consider it. Back to the drawing board and through the government red tape, we wrote an application for a SBA loan guarantee. We thought an application for a conventional bank loan was tough, this was worse.

After weeks of work, we sent the application to Washington. We were turned down. We talked with the local SBA, asked to be reconsidered, and we were turned down again. All five of us were living at our house in Southmoor Park in Southeast Denver. Missy and Louie had moved out of their home to save money and were living in Missy's old room. It was the 15th of December, our wedding anniversary, and we were at the end of our rope with seemingly no place to go. Suddenly someone said, "Why don't we call Alice Huppert, a neighbor up the street?" She was the Denver office manager for U.S. House of Representative, Patricia Schroeder. Maybe she could help. As I recall, it was around 10:00 at night when I called her, she got out of bed and listened to our problem. She finally asked why we didn't we call her sooner? She could meet with our banker and me the next day. We were told to rework the SBA application and it would be resubmitted with Representative Schroeder's support.

With David Alley's assistance, I got CHAFA's, (Colorado Housing and Finance Authority) endorsement. With Representative Schroeder's staff helping and guiding us, we rewrote and submitted the application on December 22nd. We were told not to expect any response until after the New Year holiday. I would say that was not the most pleasant Christmas we ever spent. I believe it was January 5th when I got a call from Alice Huppert. She said we had been approved! On February 3, 1989, our loan closed in the amount of $475,000.

On February 12th, with help from Pat Schroeder, Jim Lampman, Century Bank North, Kittredge Construction, my brother Ed and family, Chuck Funayama, Ron Abo Architects, Louie's brother Eugene, Jeanine Christman, Luana Steckman, John Powell, and countless others, we were set to make our dream a reality.

Luana Steckman

Luana Steckman was a friend of my daughter Melissa and an important influence in helping us understand the spiritual significance of our relationship with our new home. This is the story of Luana in Melissa's voice.

"I met Luana the summer of 1984. I was Outside Sales Manager for a hotel company known as the Granada Royale, in southeast Denver. It was the end of a very long and hot day of 'cold calls.' The way to keep my spirits up was to keep calling on businesses' until I got one of them to allow me to make my pitch. I just needed one positive meeting with a prospective client; then I could end my day on a good note.

Driving down the street I saw a sign for the headquarters of the Denver Renaissance Festival. Having recently attended the annual festival myself, I went in and the only person in the office was on the telephone. She waived me over to a comfortable chair and motioned for me to please wait. After she hung up, the woman introduced herself as Luana Steckman and offered me a cold drink of water. The temperature was hovering in the high 90s and I was parched. Gratefully sipping my cold drink, I made my presentation about hosting the Festival's out-of-town guests at my hotel. She was gracious and we hit it off. I left with a lunch meeting scheduled. We would take a tour of the hotel and chat about her clients over a nice meal. The two of us hit it off and soon became dear, dear friends. I eventually left the Granada Royale Hotel to work for several different hotel companies, ultimately losing my job due to the Savings & Loan Financial Crisis in 1987.

It was Christmas of that year, my father and I ended up standing in the unemployment line. No one was hiring and Dad and I decided to take our dire situation in hand. We would start our own business. The family had been looking at potential properties around Denver to start our own bed and breakfast. One location stood out from all the rest at the corner of 16th and Race Street.

Early in our friendship Luana had shared with me that she was a psychic. She knew things about me that I had never told anyone. I was intrigued. When I told her what our family was planning to do, she asked if she could see the house and meet the rest of the family. We set up a time on a Saturday morning to introduce Luana to my family and to our future Castle Marne.

My folks, Louie, and I had parked in the back and were walking around the north side of the building towards the front of the house. When we turned the corner there before our eyes was Luana hugging the building! She quite literally was hugging the corner of the tower. That was my parents' first impression of Luana. She turned towards us beaming! She loved the house and told us that if we wanted it, the house would help us acquire it. That was the beginning of a rich and rewarding friendship. Without Luana's positive and steadfast assurance that this amazing building was truly going to become ours, we would have lost faith many times.

Luana taught Dad how to "smudge" the house with sage and how to leave a trail of salt behind, creating a barrier of sorts, to protect the house. She explained that many lives had been lived in the house and that energy from others not of the house had entered as well. She asked us to write the "House Rules" so that we could be clear with all guests and those on this physical plane and beyond, about what was expected and what would not be tolerated. She told me to make it very clear that any uninvited or unruly guests on any plane would be shown the door without exception.

We called a meeting of the family, Luana, and all of the energies present within the house. Dad read the house rules and asked anyone who did not agree to these expectations to leave now. Luana then proceeded to move forward with the 'cleansing.' It took a few such measures over time to rid the Castle of unpleasant ghostly guests. To this day, the ethereal residents who chose to stay have been exceptional guests and are welcome for as long as they wish. It has been several of the physical guests on this plane that have given us more problems than I care to tell.

Earlier in Luana's amazing life, she had married an Egyptian doctor and had lived there for several years. She learned much about the sculpture and art of Egypt and was a font of interesting information about the symbols architect William Lang used in the building of the Castle. She explained the three successive columns of the front porch represented the stages of the blooming of the Lotus flower, a sign of welcome for centuries in the Middle East. She gave unselfishly of her time and energy to help this family bring Castle Marne to the forefront of boutique lodging in Denver.

We are forever grateful to her and her family. Luana unexpectedly passed away several years ago. My family and I count the years she was in our lives as extremely special. We miss her very much."

CHAPTER EIGHT

The Rescue
Vandals ✤ *Hurdles* ✤ *Regulators*

From 1982 through 1988, the building sat empty and for sale. A Denver law firm owned the building. At a point in time, the gas was turned off to save money, but they neglected to shut off the water. The pipes froze and burst and the water ran for weeks. The basement filled with over four feet of water. There was severe water damage to the house, especially down the main stairway and foyer.

During this time the house was vandalized to the point where there was quite simply nothing left in the house except the two first floor mantels, a mantel in a basement room when it was the owner's in-home office, the stained glass windows, half of the mantle in a second floor room and three old swamp coolers.

No furniture, furnishings, pictures, or anything that would tell you of the true history and life of the house remained. Once the "show home of the Wyman neighborhood," the historic Raymond House became known as the "big old stone house with the beautiful window." Neighbors told us they believed the house was haunted and at night they would walk across the street rather than past the mansion. The exterior of the home was dirty and in need of care. The yard was overgrown and trashy, truly a sad sight to behold.

Roughing It

One Sunday morning in late February, Louie and Melissa were bringing friends over to see our new place. It had snowed a bit during the night and a couple of sets of unknown footprints led them along the north side of the house up to the front door. As Louie and the three others opened the front door and stepped in, they heard the back door slam shut. Unbeknownst to the foursome, burglars had broken into the house. They had set up a series of crude machines with four-foot by four-foot wood and hydraulic jacks to break the wooden window-sills and steal the stained glass windows. The burglars had already started in the Formal Dining Room and were in the process of working on the six and one half foot circular stained glass peacock window on the second floor landing.

To discourage anyone else from breaking into the building, it was decided that Louie and Melissa would move into our unoccupied house that night. There was limited electricity, no running water and no heat. Construction was still in the demolition stage. They would be "roughing it."

A few months earlier, a king-sized four-poster brass and white iron bed had been purchased. They set it up in the room we named the Presidential Suite. Louie and Melissa settled in. As construction progressed, the weather warmed up. It wasn't so bad not having any heat.

Early each day before dawn and before the crew arrived, Melissa and Louie would roll out of bed, throw on some clothes and drive back across town to our family home to shower, get dressed for work, and be off to their jobs.

Let me insert an interesting note. There were about 50 big bags of asbestos and asbestos-related trash when the job was complete and we were certified asbestos-free. I was then told that those bags would be trucked to a special hazardous material dump in southern New Mexico, with my name on them. Oh, and if that dump ever closed, those bags would be delivered back to me!

Parking

David Brockway, our contractor, asked me how the property was zoned and how many parking spaces would be required? I realized this is what the doctor who wanted to restore the mansion in 1985 couldn't comply with. Unable to provide parking he had to walk away from his medical office plans.

David thought that zoning regulations probably called for a space for each of the 10 units, plus one for the on-site manager. That amounted to 11 spaces and we had three. We couldn't proceed with our project! The next day I went out to the City Building Department to check on property records of past compliance. I asked the girl at the counter for information on 1572 Race Street. She came back in about 10 minutes and told me there was not any information on that address. In fact, there didn't seem to be a building at that address. The only explanation I could think of at that moment was that no previous owners had taken out building permits for their projects. I quickly explained to her that there was a really big stone house at that location and this was very important to me. Well, she came back with the department head, Chuck Funayama. I explained my situation to him and he seemed sympathetic to my problem. He told me yes, we would need to provide 11 parking spaces and suggested I make an appointment with the Denver Board of Appeals, which had the authority to deal with this sort of zoning matter.

I dutifully called and got an appointment that Friday to appear before the board. Thursday morning, I got a call from Chuck Funayama, who asked to meet with me before the appointment. I dropped everything and went to see him. We went into his office and he closed the door. He said that he was intrigued with my situation, and had begun digging into old dusty rules and regulations. Somewhere he found an old still valid, regulation that dealt with "parking credits." The long and short of it was that the rule said if the building had been used continuously over a period of years as a housing unit, that parking credits are accumulated for each year, which can be used against parking space requirements. I swallowed hard and asked how many credits the property now had and how many parking spaces would I have to provide. He smiled and said there were more than enough credits and I would have to provide zero; none at all. He smiled at me and said, "Jim, what you want to do is going to be wonderful for that house and neighborhood." He signed the release form and wished me well.

Kitchen

In the process of applying for our B&B license, we were told we could not open without a Health Department Inspected commercial kitchen, complete with externally vented exhaust hoods, and commercial kitchen fire abatement systems. Our 12-feet by 8-feet space would not allow for all of this. The National Register people as well as the Denver Landmark Commission said we couldn't make the necessary changes to the exterior of the building to accommodate the exterior venting requirements for a commercial kitchen. The Waste Water Department said the existing sewer wouldn't accommodate commercial kitchen effluent without a grease trap. Oh yes, and we would have to make the kitchen larger.

We were stymied again! I argued and protested to no avail. That's when David Brockway stepped up and reminded the city folks that several years before, when he was involved in building a restaurant in the basement of the old historic Ice House in lower downtown Denver. They faced the same venting problems we were dealing with. He reminded them that they were able to work out an agreement that they would not prepare or offer any food that "would produce grease or gaseous vapors." They submitted sample menus that did not include any fried foods and offered to sign documents attesting to all of the above. I said I would agree to the same restrictions and sign any documents they felt were necessary to allow us to move ahead with our project. They finally grudgingly agreed. And yes, as we were not producing any grease, we didn't have to install a grease trap.

As a side note though, after we opened, a Waste Water Inspector came out every month and climbed down in the sewer in the alley to inspect our sewer drainage to be sure we were not sneaking grease down the sewer. After a few months of finding no grease, he said that he would not be seeing us again. We understand that this unique arrangement is no longer authorized by the city.

Windows

We thought we were out of the woods. Back in the 1920s, the house was converted to apartments. All of the upstairs units had private balconies. The third floor unit on the front of the house presented a special problem because one of the windows in the room was removed and replaced by a door that originally accessed a balcony, which no longer existed. We told the Building Department we were, of course, going to take out the door and replace it with a window. The Landmark Commission said we would have to exactly match the original rusticated rhyolite stone windowsill, wooden double-hung frame and decorative stone below it.

We found a window shop that could make the window as needed to satisfy the Commission. Insofar as the stonework was concerned, the quarries down in Castle Rock had been closed for many years and we couldn't find the rhyolite to make the match. Up stepped our contractor who suggested we make a mold of the remaining adjacent original sill and cast a replacement of aggregate stone which would match the original.

The commission would have none of it. Brock knew of a stonemason who had done this sort of thing before. Finally, the Commission agreed on letting him try and they would decide whether or not to approve it. It was amazing to watch the workmen prepare the mold. It took two-three weeks to make this big white blob mold on the front of the house and let it dry. Finally, when it was ready, it took six of us to carefully pry the mold off of the house and lower it to the ground. It must have weighed 300-400 pounds. It took three tries to cast an imitation rusticated rhyolite windowsill that satisfied the Commission. We were getting closer.

Stoop

One of the Building Department employees, I'll call him Les, was determined to make my life difficult. He said city code required that all nonconforming objects in the public right-of-way have an annually-renewed Certificate of Compliance, which excluded the city from any liability. The large piece of rock at the front curb, known as the carriage mounting stone, and the stone hitching post, were nonconforming objects in the Public Right of Way. I argued and complained to no avail.

I had gotten to know Dr. Charles Brantigan, a prominent surgeon and historian, who lived in William Lang's last designed home. He had been told the same story about a mounting stone in front of his home. We began to make the rounds. Finally, a supervisor in the Building Department agreed that the certificate wasn't necessary.

Fence Points

Les then came up with another problem. The beautiful handwrought iron fence, dating to around 1900, atop a low wall along the sidewalk, was in the city's right of way by two inches. It had little sharp points that were a public hazard and had to be dealt with. Being in the public right of way, it would require a Certificate of Compliance. Whenever I was down to the Building Department, he would somehow find me and suggest a solution he had thought up for my problem. Once it was to buy a lot of small metal balls and weld them onto the sharp points, which would solve everything. Except it would be a huge amount of work, look like hell, and the Landmark Commission wouldn't allow it.

Another time he said all I had to do was unbolt the fence sections and turn them upside down and re-bolt them with the points going downward. It would also be a huge amount of work, was a dumb idea, and the Landmark Commission wouldn't allow it. Finally, he put his foot down and said I had to apply for a Certificate of Compliance, which would absolve the city of any responsibility when some little child climbing on the fence, slipped or injured themselves. By now, it was getting well into June and we were rushing to finish and open for business. He threatened to file a complaint and seriously stall things. So I said, "you win, I will grind down the points." I borrowed a heavy-duty grinder and very carefully ground down the points ever so slightly. It was barely enough to notice, but it satisfied Les.

Handicap Ramps

We had one more hoop to jump through. A city traffic engineer came along and said I had to install handicap ramps at my street corner. There was a city-funded program to install corner handicap ramps, but our neighborhood wasn't scheduled until the following year. Ours needed to be done or we could not open for business. As I recall, because of the slope and angle, they would have to be 22-feet long and would cost $7,000-$8,000. If we could have waited until the next year, it would have been free. It had to be done right away. I had made a couple of friends in city hall and I called them for help. A week or so went by and I got a call from the guy in charge of the city-funded program for installing handicap ramps. He had heard my story and said that he would be able to rearrange the schedule of installations so that our corner would be moved up to the top of the list. Wonderful news, but they were still going to be 22-feet long and still going to look like hell.

A few days later, my son Riley and I were walking down to Pete's Kitchen for lunch, when I noticed the steep slope and shortness of the handicap ramp on the corner of Colfax and Race streets. After lunch, and thinking more about it, Riley and I went back down to the corner with a couple of two-by-four pieces of wood, a level, yard stick, tape measure and a couple of clamps. We clamped the two-by-four pieces together, carried them out into Colfax traffic, leveled them and measured the height and angle of the ramp. It was less than half of what they said we were required to have. To make a long story short, we got a shortened, free ramp that looked fine and was done in six weeks.

Update to April 22, 2017. We found a flyer on our door knob from the City, informing us that the handicap ramps on our corner and thousands more around the city, were not in ADA compliance. They would be rebuilt next week at today's standard, at no cost to us. It seems the ADA had gone around the city measuring ramps. Then they sued the City forcing compliance. Some days you just don't know.

CHAPTER NINE

The Renovation

Fleur-de-lis ✢ Furnishings ✢ Phelyx

A lot of stuff had to be cleaned out before we could really get down to the restoration and renovation. We removed the old boiler, water damaged lath and plaster walls, old carpet, original knob and tube electrical wiring, lead water and drain piping, and miles of telephone wire. These were just some of what filled up a 40-cubic yard dumpster every week.

Decorating

Fleur-de-lis

The old water damaged lath and plaster walls from the second floor down to the Foyer had to be demolished. The small plaster cast fleur-de-lis that had decorated the walls for over a century couldn't be saved. I saw the architectural and historical integrity of my building going into the dumpster. I had to do something. I saved a few of the unbroken castings, took them to a craft store and asked them how I could reproduce them. Not a problem. They sold me some Plaster of Paris, latex rubber and told me how to make a mold. After several tries I made a mold that worked! I began casting fleur-de-lis that looked just like the original. Over the next several months I produced over 400 of them. After the sheetrock was hung, and before the walls were painted, we hot melt-glued my new fleur-de-lis back on the walls as they had originally been. They looked great.

About 15 years later, I realized that the plaster cast fleur-de-lis had originally been gilded, not painted the same color as the walls. Using very tiny brushes, a bunch of us spent one entire summer painting every one of the new 396 fleur-de-lis, as well as every one of the original first floor castings that had not been damaged.

They looked so good that I set about to gild the "pressed plaster" decorations on the ceiling and frieze of the foyer. As I learned, "pressed plaster" decorating sometimes was used as a substitute for hand-painted ceiling art. Plaster was troweled on the ceiling and frieze and then a carved wooden die was pressed into the plaster as it set. The pattern would be replicated all around the frieze and ceiling creating an amazing two-dimensional effect. Looking at the 1890 photo in the foyer, you will notice "pressed plaster" art that replaced the original hand-painted ceiling and frieze.

Phelyx

All of this brings me to perhaps the most amazing Innkeeper we ever had. We had been open four or five years, when a young man by the name of Phelyx Hopkins came to our door looking for a job. His name was actually Richard, but you know how artsy folks can be. He was a starving artist who wasn't able to support himself as an artist. We hired him as an Innkeeper. He and I would often talk about the 1890 photos around the house, especially the picture to the right of the front door. He kept saying "I can do that; I can replicate that ceiling and frieze art. Just give me a chance." Well, I applied for a matching grant the very first year casino gambling money was distributed. We were awarded the grant and Phelyx was on the way to reproducing what you now see in the Front and Back Parlor ceilings and frieze. Oh yes, it covered the boiler water pipes as well. The process was as amazing as the finished product. He took the picture, had it blown up to the dimension of the frieze, which is the portion of the wall above the picture rail to the ceiling. Mr. Webster defines a frieze as "a decoration or series of decorations forming an ornamental band around a room."

Phelyx then separated the design into four individual patterns making up the whole four-color project. Then he cut by hand, four stencils out of clear plastic material with an Exacto Knife, one for each color of the finished painting. He would tape the first stencil up and trace the pattern on the wall with a pencil, proceeding all around the room. Then he would start back at the beginning and hand paint in the penciled pattern all around the room. He did this four times, each screen a different color. Then on the fifth time around he painted the border on the ceiling, creating the work of art you see today.

The hot water heating pipes were another problem. We realized the pipes themselves had to be painted, not just the wall behind them. He couldn't attain a dimensional view of the pattern on the pipes to match the painting on the wall behind. So I stood back about 12-15 feet and directed his painting so that it very nearly blends in and becomes the same. His work gave us a very unique step back in time to an era of attention to detail and opulence. The entire project took over six months to complete.

Upon finishing the Parlor project, Phelyx turned to the Dining Room ceiling. The original 1890 photograph shows a striking example of the Orientalism design craze that swept America in the 1880s and 1890s. In our house, Chinese or Japanese flowers were depicted. It occurred to me that it would be more interesting if we featured Colorado flowers. So Phelyx and I looked at a Colorado flower book and substituted like-appearing flowers. We started with our state flower, the Columbine, over the door into the Back Parlor. To create the semi-circle pattern, he made a giant four foot compass to accomplish the rounded effect at each end. Through freehand painting, he created a uniquely distinctive Dining Room ceiling unlike any other in the city. Phelyx left us shortly after virtually completing the Dining Room ceiling. It was actually about 98% done, but don't bother trying to find the 2%. He left us to take a job at Lannie's Clock Tower Night Club, in the old Daniels and Fisher Tower basement, performing table magic. He is a very talented magician, as well as an artist, and a friend.

Furnishings

Our dream B&B was underway. Now was the time to start thinking about decorating and furnishing it. We really didn't know where to start or what we wanted the interior to look like. After a lot of searching around, we just started calling on wholesale suppliers of hotel and motel furniture. One day Diane and I were meeting with a supplier and having a very hard time explaining what we wanted to achieve. He didn't know much, if anything, about bed and breakfasts, and wasn't really interested in anything but Motel 6-style furniture and fixtures. We were getting frustrated and about to leave, when we heard a voice from another room calling out "for God's sakes, Harry you don't get it. Let me talk to them, I know what they want!" Around a corner came a kind of hippy-looking woman who introduced herself as Jeanine Christman. She lived in Durango and operated "Jeanine's Studio of Design." She was in Denver, calling on designers and just happened to overhear us. Kind of makes you wonder doesn't it?

Jeanine, Diane and I, went out to lunch together and we soon realized she would be the one to get us started. A couple of weeks later, Diane and Melissa drove to Durango and spent several days with Jeanine at her studio. She was able to put our dreams and thoughts down on paper and get us on track. Again, we were all at the right place at the right time. Jeanine became our decorator, consultant, and friend. We couldn't have done it without her!

We acquired a special piece of furniture from The Clarko Hotel, which was located immediately to the south of the old Mammoth Gardens property, facing Colfax. The hotel was torn down in 1990, but a mantelpiece, now in our Tower Room, was saved before demolition and is the last reminder of The Clarko Hotel.

CHAPTER TEN

The Grand Opening
Five Months Later ✤ Celebration

Colorado Day

August 1st is Colorado Day. August 1st was our deadline date to open. With less than five-and-one-half months before August 1, the family and hearty friends worked long hours, seven days a week. David Brockway, our General Contractor, supervised the construction crew ensuring the project stayed on time. Our extended family and friends worked evenings and weekends striping paint, refinishing original hardwood, and cleaning up after the construction crews every night. I hung all the wallpaper.

During construction well-wishers would stop by to see what was going on. If the family was not on site, the construction workers had them sign a guest book. As August 1st drew near, the pressure to open on time was on everyone's mind. A grand opening party was planned to mark the big day. Neighbors, family, well-wishers, strangers, inspectors, and former owners of the house were invited to the celebration. We continued to move forward as we pointed to opening on August 1st, 1989, exactly one year from loan closing, August 1st, 1988. We made it!

After two all-nighters decorating, making beds, setting up furniture, washing windows and organizing the kitchen, the opening day arrived. Our friend and my fraternity brother, Ralph Hegsted set up his Dixie-land Jazz band in the front yard. He has not missed being here for Colorado Day in 27 years. With food and beverages, the family dressed in Victorian costumes and welcomed guests for the first of Castle Marne's August 1st Colorado Day Parties.

Everyone gathered out on the lawn in front of the three-story tower for the "Official Christening" of the Castle Marne Bed & Breakfast. Melissa gripped the neck of a bottle of champagne in her hand and raised it to break the bottle against the rusticated stone of the Castle. "Boink," went the bottle. Melissa moved to strike the bottle again. "Boink," the intact bottle bounced off. Instead of breaking the bottle, Melissa was chipping the 100-year-old-stone wall! After several attempts, finally the bottle broke, spraying those standing nearby with chips of stone and champagne.

Every August 1st since, the family celebrates the Castle Marne's birthday. The annual event still has Ralph's Dixie-Land Jazz Band, birthday cakes, popcorn wagon, and cotton candy machine for neighbors, friends and well-wishers.

CHAPTER ELEVEN

The Mansion Exterior

Rhyolite ✢ Lotus, Orb and Scepter ✢ Upside Down Tree

Official Designations

On November 21, 1974, the Marne/ Wilbur Raymond House was listed on The National Register of Historic Places, inventory number 5DV123.

In 1974 The Marne/Wilbur Raymond House was officially listed as Denver Registered Landmark Building, Number 71.

Located in Denver's Wyman Historic District, Ordinance No. 774 series of 1993, officially designated on October 19, 1993.

1997, officially listed on the: Du Pont National Register of American Castles

January 25, 1995 Selection of Castle Marne as a U.S. Small Business Administration, Denver District, "SUCCESS STORY."

What does the Castle Marne B&B have in common with the magnificent Trinity Methodist Church at 18th and Broadway in downtown Denver? Strange you would ask.

One of the most prominent building stones used in the Front Range is a lovely light tan and gray-to-pinkish volcanic rock found on mesa tops in Douglas County, commonly called Castle Rock Rhyolite. It graces the exterior of many Denver area buildings, from business blocks such as the Ghost Building, churches such as Trinity Methodist and residences such as Castle Marne.

Rhyolite

Rhyolite is sometimes mistaken for limestone because of its light color and fine-grained texture. Like granite, it is mainly quartz, mica and feldspar. Unlike granite, rhyolite is extrusive, formed above ground rather than below ground. It originated some 35-million years ago in a highly eruptive center in the present Sawatch Mountains of Chaffee County in western Colorado. The material was erupted as airborn ash, which settled over vast areas of Park, Teller, and Douglas Counties. Fossils are preserved in rhyolite deposits of the Florissant Fossil Beds National Monument in Teller County.

The first quarry was opened in 1872 near Castle Rock, Colorado (incidentally, the cap stone of Castle Rock is rhyolite). Eventually there were five quarries operating between Castle Rock and Palmer Lake. The Denver and Rio Grande Railroad served the quarries, shipping stone to Colorado Springs, Denver, Cheyenne, and as far away as Kansas City. Business boomed, and thousands of tons were shipped by 1874. A large community of skilled workers, some from Sweden, worked the quarries. Many of their descendants still live around Castle Rock. The rhyolite quarries thrived until the silver crash of 1893. As the depression abated, the use of concrete and brick, which were much cheaper building materials, signaled the end of the Castle Rock Rhyolite era.

Rhyolite is truly amazing, it carves and rusticates very well; it is lightweight compared to sandstone or granite. Interestingly it has a 2-3R insulation rating. Standing in front of our Castle Marne, you are struck by the extent and complexity of the hand carvings gracing the building, particularly around the windows of the Turret.

Pillars

Our friend Luana Steckman, lived in Egypt for several years. She gave special meaning to the three capitals forming the pillars supporting the front porch. She told us that the carvings represent the Lotus plant, which in Eastern cultures signifies welcome. They are welcoming you to our Castle. The capital atop the column on your right represents the Lotus plant. The center more complex capital represents the Lotus plant in bud. The most complex carving to your left represents the Lotus plant in full bloom, completing your welcome to our Castle Marne. Welcome, Bienvenu!

Symbols of Royalty

While we are talking about the Front Porch, note the ceiling light fixture. The lamp was part of the Aladdin Theatre, built in 1924 at Colfax and Vine, just a block south of the Castle. It was Denver's premier 1920s movie cinema. It featured a beautiful mosque-like dome. It was Denver's most beautiful movie house. This is one of only a few decorative lamps that didn't get bulldozed into the landfill when the theatre was demolished in 1988. The theater was replaced by Walgreens Drug store. This Aladdin's lamp was given to me for use and safekeeping.

Note the large round carving atop the highest peak on the front façade, representing an orb, along with the large vertical member beside the downspout representing a scepter, hence the Scepter and Orb, symbols of our Castle's royalty.

Additions

Note the two large third floor windows on the front. Originally there was no glass in the openings; they were part of a balcony room off of the third floor Ballroom. Here gentlemen could step out for a smoke, and a breath of fresh air. In the first floor Parlor, you can see a 1890 photograph showing this feature.

The first floor building extension you see on the south side is interesting. When the building became an apartment house in 1919, the original small iron and glass conservatory was replaced by the addition you now see, housing the kitchen and the Conservatory guest room. In the Parlor you will see 1890 photographs of this addition. Amazingly, they moved the room you see in the photograph stone-by-stone to its present location.

A local architect commented on another addition, "The one story staid addition to the rear of the building is constructed of stone, which nearly matches the original building. It is evident this addition was not designed by Mr. Lang, as it is squat, square and tends toward being squalid. Over the years small conveniences have been appended to the old place, balconies bespangle the sides of the house like leeches. The exuberant life which cavorts over, around and through it is the result, not of good planning, but of human participation."

Peacock Window

The exterior view of the six-feet by six-feet stained and leaded crystal glass Peacock Window is a trademark of the mansion, crafted by Clarence Watkins in 1888.

Langisms

Immediately below the Peacock Window on the north side, is a doorway and window, featuring a typical Langism. "Adjacent arches sharing a baroque bouquet concealing what is known in the architectural trade as a 'whoops.' Arches have traditionally sprung from what is known as a 'spring line.' Since the two openings beneath the arches under discussion were placed too close to each other, the accumulation of masonry above the arches precluded a nice neat spring line." Mr. Lang was never one to let tradition interfere.

The nine-fluted chimney is unique, unlike any other we have seen in Mr. Lang's work. To the right of the front door above the main window is a stone arch with two stained and leaded glass windows that defy structural aesthetics. The structural theory behind an arch is that it is a self-supporting system of spanning openings through the use of small pieces of masonry. The topmost piece of masonry is called a keystone. It is the stone that completes the arch and expresses its theory. Lang neatly places a column under that critical unit, thus at a stroke denying the arch and titillating our senses. Architects call it a whimsy. The triple dental around the balcony is well-defined and in excellent condition.

Home Office

The formal step-up access from 16th Avenue to the doorway on the north side of the Castle is an early adaptation of a now accepted feature, the home office. Think about it, there are really two formal entrances to the Castle, the front entrance off of Race Street into the Foyer and first floor, and the side entrance into the downstairs home office. At the bottom of the stairs was a waiting area, comfortable office space with a corner brick fireplace and stone mantel. The oak doors, rosettes, and chamfered beadboard paneling in the stairway are equal in quality to the woodwork in the rest of the house. Callers would have had access to the owner in his downstairs office, where he could conduct business without disturbing the regular functions of the household.

Fence

Be sure to study the hand-wrought iron decorative fence on the short wall along the sidewalk. The intricate swirling pattern was all forged, wrought, hammered, and formed by hand. The swirling design is a delicate contrast to the boldness of the mansion's architecture, unlike anything else we have seen in the city. The large Carriage Mounting Stone at the curb is uniquely Victorian. There would have been another smaller stone on top of the larger. Its purpose was quite simply to allow ladies to step out of their horse drawn carriage onto the stone with ease and grace while hopefully not showing too much ankle. The stone hitching post requires no explanation. One can stand and gaze at the fence, the yard and façade at length and never comprehend all of its uniqueness.

Upside Down Tree

This leads me to perhaps the most unique urban legend we treasure so much, the famous or infamous Upside Down Tree. On the north side of the building there was a large mostly dead tree, which overshadowed the view of the house and needed to be cut down.

Neighbors told me that this was the famous upside down tree, which had been featured in Robert Ripley's Believe it or Not newspaper feature. The story goes that owner Lyle Holland planted the tree. Subsequently, for some unknown reason, the tree was dug up and replanted, upside down. Amazingly the tree survived, its branches becoming its roots and the roots becoming the branches of the tree. I have been told that biologically, this is impossible. It was a miracle! The branches did actually have a very unusual root like configuration.

We were told that neighborhood children would come over to bounce and play on the unusual limbs near to the ground. The story was known and loved throughout the neighborhood, and that the new owner of the "big old stone house on the corner with the beautiful window," was going to cut the famous tree down. I tried very diligently to ascertain the truth of the story. The limited contact I could make with the "Believe it or not" people was less than helpful. At that time they had a summer "Believe it or not" Museum in Estes Park. I made a trip there to talk to them. They said it might have happened, but that their records were not complete. They said there had been thousands and thousands (actually over 100,000) features printed and they couldn't say yes or no that this did in fact appear in print. I was told that the company had had its headquarters in Canada, but was relocating to Orlando, Florida. Shortly after that, while attending an Independent Innkeepers Association (IIA) meeting in Florida, I called on them hoping to get some resolution, but was greeted with the same "could have been" answers.

As the tree was dead, the old grouch cut it down.

Quoted Descriptions

A friend of mine, Jack Murphy was Curator of Geology at the Denver Museum of Nature and Science. He wrote this for us:

"Another William Lang landmark building is the remarkable Raymond House at 1572 Race Street. An elaborate 1889 mansion once owned by John T. Mason, a founder and trustee of the Museum.

According to one report, the original owner, Wilbur Raymond, commissioned the house to be built for $40,000 on land valued at $15,000. He lived in the house for less than 2 years. He was forced to sell it in 1893, the year of the Silver Crash. If you stroll by this historic building, you see the Eclectic style at its best with unparalleled workmanship in rock work, carvings and stained glass."

Jack told me that the Castle is perhaps only one of half dozen homes in Denver completely built of rhyolite.

Our Castle Marne was featured in the Denver Chapter of the American Institute of Architects' 1995 House tour. I am very pleased and proud of their brochure's description:

"Style: Richardsonian Eclecticism

Constructed in 1889 by Wilbur S. Raymond, the Castle Marne is truly one of Denver's great architectural legacies. The Castle Marne is the work of William Lang, one of Denver's most prolific and gifted residential designers of the late 19th century. Note the eclectic Richardsonian massing and detailing of the mansion

– the heavily rusticated stonework juxtaposed with the refined, delicate elements of glass and fenestration.

Like so many Capitol Hill Residences, the Castle Marne has changed ownership many times, and ultimately rescued from severe disrepair. The current incarnation of the structure as the ten-room Castle Marne Bed and Breakfast, a function which preserves both the architecture and elegance of the mansion. While visiting the Mansion, note the entry foyer woodwork, the stained glass on the stair to the second floor, and the fireplace detailing of the first floor parlor/living room. Also note that despite having stood abandoned for years prior to renovation, subject to water and wind damage, the exterior stone load bearing walls are perfectly plumb and true, with virtually no visible deterioration."

We all agree, it is indeed a remarkably elegant building.

Our William Lang designed the castle rock rhyolite mansion.

CHAPTER TWELVE

The First Floor Tour

Welcome ✤ Lang Bust ✤ Green Man

Foyer - Moorish Fretwork

The wood fret work that can be seen on the first floor landing (what's left of it), is all that remains of the magnificent Moorish Fret that graced the mansion when it was built. The 1890 photos show it in its glowing glory.

About 14 years ago, late one evening I received a phone call from a very excited man named Paul Tucker, calling from Pennsylvania. He asked if I owned the Raymond House, I replied, "yes." He then went into a fascinating story of researching unusual wood fret made by Moses Ransom back in the 1880s. He was now trying to re-patent the unique manufacturing process for the product. For some time he had been going to his public library researching pictures of Victorian mansions all across the country, to study their fret work. He found the Lang portfolio (online) in the Denver Public Library. In that portfolio he found the same 1890 photos we have here in our mansion, showing the fantastic wood fret work around all the first floor. He said these were designs he had never seen, and our Moorish Fret was the farthest west he knew of it having been sold.

He was so excited I could hardly understand him. He asked if I would send him detailed photographs of all the frets in our house. When I told him it was all gone, none left. I think he covered the receiver and cried. He finally came back on the line and apologized for taking my time, etc. Then I remembered there was one piece of the broken-up fret left on the stair landing. I said I would send him a photo of it. I did, and never heard from him again.

Moorish Fretwork was invented by Moses Y. Ransom in Cleveland, Ohio in the 1880s. It was a unique method of woodworking that weaves milled spiral rods of opposite chirality into many different ornamental patterns and designs. Introduced in 1885, Ransom's in-

vention involved cross-threading machined wooden spiral moldings, creating both right-handed and left-handed moldings. He discovered that he could "weave" or interlace them into patterns that resembled the geometries of Islamic design. The silhouettes of Ransom's designs reveal negative and positive regions that create a fretwork or lattice structure, hence Ransom's moniker of Moorish Fretwork.

Unfortunately, Ransom's work wasn't available until the tail-end of the Orientalism design craze in America and only enjoyed about ten years of popularity from 1888 to 1895. During those ten years though, Moorish Fretwork in both ornamental lattice screens and in furniture graced many of the most stylish homes of the Victorian era in the United States, including our own Castle Marne.

The mantel in the Foyer was built especially for the mansion. The mirror mirrors the shape of the Peacock Window, being a circle with its base cut off that is the architectural signature of William Lang the mansion's architect.

Note the 1890 photo to the right of the front door, especially the doorway Moorish Fret and the ceiling/frieze painting. All of the stairway, paneling, trim, and floor is original quarter sawn golden oak. The front door and hardware are original. The original leaded glass window was destroyed in the early 1980s and replaced with a pane of LOF automobile safety glass. The hot water radiator is original to the late 1890s, when central heat was added.

On the wall beside the desk, note that the fleur-de-lis are slightly different than the rest in the foyer and up the stairs.

Take note of the spandrel or fret work in the doorway going into the front parlor. The spandrel or fret you see today is not original; I added it after we opened.

Originally there was a door from the Foyer into the Back Parlor when there were two rooms, the Front or Formal Parlor and the Family Parlor separated by a wall (note the photo beside the Grandfather Clock).

The Parlor

The front or Formal Parlor, as it was in 1890, is pictured on the west wall to your right, along with an exterior photograph of the Raymond family standing on the front porch of their new home. This is as far as Denver had built by 1889. Note there are no houses pictured to the east. York Street was the city limit.

The entry into the Turret clearly shows a remarkable example of Moorish Fret, called "The sun and the old man in the moon." On closer examination you will see in the upper right, the "rays of the sun." In the upper left you will see a crescent moon with the silhouette of the face of the "old man in the moon" in it. Mr. Tucker told me he had seldom seen this design; it was very rare indeed.

In the Turret, if you look carefully you will see the Samovar for hot water, and the table set for Afternoon Tea.

William Lang Bust

About 20 years ago, a local sculptor named Tom Cerillo came to our door with an amazing request. He told me that he and his business partner, Thomas Jay Warren, had been awarded a contract from the State of New Jersey to design and construct the state's new Korean War Memorial. His partner would be coming to Denver to complete his part of the sculpture, and he wanted him to stay for a month at our Castle Marne, and to experience the special sense of William Lang, the architect. Tom was a great admirer of William Lang and his remarkable architectural and artistic talent.

After arranging the reservation details for the month stay, I asked how the charges would be handled. Tom asked me if we would be up to a "trade out." I asked what he had to "trade out," and he replied that his partner would sculpt a life size bust of William Lang and Tom would cast it in bronze. I quickly agreed, and the bust you see in our front parlor is the wonderful result.

Tom told me that he would make the wood base for the bust. I had told him that I had already planned to place Mr. Lang's bust at the window in the Front Parlor. The day finally arrived when Tom brought the completed bust of Mr. Lang to his new home, and placed it on the stand. It was covered with a beautiful velvet cloth. We opened a bottle of champagne to toast the event as Tom ceremoniously pulled the velvet cloth off. We were so very proud to have the only bronze bust of Denver's most prolific and gifted architect right here in our castle. With a sly grin, Tom told us that Mr. Lang would occasionally tire of facing into the parlor, so when he built the wooden base, he included a "swivel" feature so that we could simply spin the bust around so that Mr. Lang could look outside for a change of view.

Queen Victoria

To the left of the turret you see a most unusual framed lithograph, with a delightful story. Four or five years after we opened, we had a guest named Dr. David Goode from London. He was in town attending a seminar at the Museum of Natural History on the subject of Urban Ecology.

At breakfast one morning, he began to gently rag me about being a Victorian mansion, but we had no pictures of Queen Victoria, only the "unfinished" portrait of George Washington staring across the table at him. He said, "In her early years you should know she was a strikingly beautiful young woman."

Taking a bit of mock affront, I said, "Please no offense intended, but I have only seen pictures of Her Highness where she quite resembles a lump of mashed potatoes."

With tongue in cheek he responded, "If I find a picture of Queen Victoria as an attractive woman and I buy it will you hang it here in the Castle Marne?"

We laughed and joked a bit, and of course I said "yes," and that I would give her a place of prominence and I would pay for it.

Over a year went by and I hadn't thought about it again, when early one morning the telephone rang, it was Dr. Goode. He said he was calling from an art gallery in Brighton, England, and had found a picture of the Queen that he knew I would like, and could he buy it per our agreement. What else could I say but of course, and oh, what was the cost? He said the cost was 200 Pounds Sterling. He would be coming through Denver in a couple of months and would bring the picture with him.

Well as you can see he was spot-on and I was wrong. He told me the lithograph was made shortly after her inauguration on 20 June, 1837 at the age of 18. It is certified by the "Office of Antiquities" as authentic. Her Highness has brightened our "Victorian" inn ever since.

Original authenticated color lithograph of Queen Victoria, 1832, being welcomed into our Castle Marne.

Dolphins

On the upper portion of the mantel in the Front Parlor, you see the figures of two fish-like creatures; they are carved stylized dolphins. Throughout history, when after long months at sea, sailors were welcomed into port by dolphins swimming along beside their ships. The dolphin became an international symbol of welcome. The dolphins on our mantel welcome you into our Castle Marne.

The Green Man

The Green Man welcomes you to our castle as well, along with the Lotus carvings on the front porch capitols.

The face of the Green Man is found on both sides of the lower portions of the hand carved fireplace mantel in the parlor. We believe the mantel was carved in England and somehow made its way to Denver to be given a place of honor in our Castle Marne. The stone surrounding the fireplace opening is onyx, from Oaxaca, Mexico. The Green Man motif has many variations. Found in ancient cultures around the world, the Green Man is often related to natural vegetative deities springing up in different cultures throughout the ages. Primarily it is interpreted as a symbol of rebirth, or "renaissance," representing the cycle of growth each spring. His appearance is consistent, but never the same. His facial "hair" is green growing leaves, flowers, and vines. Our Green Man's beard trails all the way to the floor.

Some years ago, Diane and I were visiting her brother Kenny and his wife Margaret in Oaxaca, Mexico. We were touring the central square of the city. Around the square were three Catholic churches and the Governor's Palace, all dating to the 15th century. We were standing in front of one of the churches listening to the guide (she spoke very good English), when I looked at the facade of the church and there was the face of the Green Man carved in the stone. I nudged Diane and whispered, "There is the Green Man." The guide overheard me and we had a wonderful discussion of the meaning of the Green Man from her point of view, as well as mine.

Born in the ancient pagan times of Mother Earth, questioning and seeking answers to natural phenomena effecting and surrounding them.

The Green Man became one of many pagan symbolisms that made its way into early Christian beliefs and recognition as an icon in early architectural renderings. He is the symbol of the eternal cycle of Nature, the mysterious figure who dies and is reborn each year. He is a part of interwoven beliefs and customs associated with ploughing and sowing, with harvest and the autumn slaughter of beasts – the seeming death of Nature in winter, followed by the miracle of rebirth in the Spring. To the medieval Christian mind he became a symbol of rebirth after death.

The Green Man can be found in churches, chapels and cathedrals all across Europe. He dances in May Day processions in Britain. He appears on temple walls in India and in churches in Borneo. He is Osiris, Dionysius, Odin, Tamuz. He is still very much with us today. He is a symbol of rebirth in May marking the beginning of new life in the spring as we celebrate the rebirth of Christ at Easter. As old as four thousand years, the Green Man has become intertwined in folk days with "Jack o' the Green," "John Barleycorn," and even "Robin Hood." Each and every "Green Man" is different in the way the craftsman or the age interprets him, but the message is always the same— there is life after death. So many amazingly designed images of the same icon, created all over the world long before communication could have influenced the earliest copies bear testament to a strong and long-held belief.

Green Men are found in so many places once you start looking. To be so widespread in comparatively modern cathedrals as St. Paul's and Notre Dame is an indication how closely he was linked to Christianity at that time. Green Men can be found all around the world. In France they are in Rouen Cathedral, in Bourges, Chartres, Sees, Auxerre, and many smaller churches.

In Germany there are many more and in England they can be found in Exeter, Ely, Winchester, Lichfield and in hundreds of parish churches. The Chapter House at Southwell Minster has a dozen or more—but never a likeness of Christ or the Virgin.

In Roslin Chapel, (famous in Dan Brown's book, *The Da Vinci Code*) a Templar church south of Edinburgh, there are reputed to be over a hundred Green Men – but they say you will never be able to count them all correctly! Where other pagan symbols were crushed under the weight of iconoclastic Christianity, the sacred tree, the vine, and the oak survived along with the Green Man, symbol of rebirth, irrepressible vitality, and love of nature.

He will be with us forever. He gives us hope and comfort. He welcomes you to our Castle Marne.

Green Man Bookends

During a conversation with Tom Cerillo, who cast the bust of William Lang, the subject of the Green Man came up. I mentioned that someday I would like to have a casting of the face of the Green Man. I didn't think about it again, until a young woman came to the door

telling me that Tom Cerillo sent her. She came in and set about casting a mold of the Green Man. She didn't know why Tom wanted the mold. For Christmas that year Tom gave us the set of bronze bookends you see in the Parlor; the face of the Green Man. Thank you, Tom.

Green Man bookends carved in bronze by Denver artist J. Tom Carrillo. Cast from parlor mantel.

Pictures

To the left of the mantel, you see a large pastoral oil painting of a herder and his sheep. Note all of the sheep have a front hoof raised. The artist is Clementine Saue, dated 1915, and titled "End of the Day." It has been in our family for many years. I have been unable to locate any information about her.

Note the two old photographs hanging by the door out to the veranda. The upper photograph shows the mansion under construction in 1888. Neither the Peacock Window nor the front door had been installed.

The lower picture is Colonel James H. Platt, the second owner of the mansion.

Army Plaque

The round wooden plaque on the wall to the right of the sideboard is a wonderful story.

The 3rd Army Division was activated in November 1917, seven months after the American entry into World War I. Eight months later, it saw combat for the first time in France on the Western Front. At midnight on 14 July 1918, the division earned lasting distinction. Engaged in the Aisne-Marne Offensive as a member of the American Expeditionary Force (AEF) to Europe, the division was protecting the French capital of Paris with a position on the banks of the Marne River. The 7th Machine Gun Battalion of the 3rd Division rushed to Château-Thierry amid retreating French troops and held the Germans back at the Marne River. When flanking units retreated, then Division Commander, Major General Joseph Dickman, told our French allies "Nous Resterons La - We shall remain here." While surrounding units retreated, the 3rd Division remained steadfast throughout the Second Battle of the Marne, and Colonel Ulysses G. McAlexander's dogged defense earned the 3rd Division its nickname as the "Rock of the Marne," also known as the "Marne Men." General John Joseph "Black Jack" Pershing, Commander-in-Chief of the AEF on the Western Front, called this stand "one of the most brilliant pages in the annals of military history."

A dear friend and fraternity brother of mine fought in the Korean War and was assigned to the 3rd Infantry Division, earning The Purple Heart. When he learned how the name Marne was chosen by Adele Van Cise, he made the plaque, using a shoulder patch from one of his uniforms. The story and the plaque have a very special meaning to us.

One morning at breakfast someone asked about the plaque and its meaning. As I was telling about the "Rock of the Marne" and "The Marne Men," I was interrupted by a young woman who respectfully said, "Excuse me Jim, I am 3rd Infantry. We don't use the term "Marne Men" any longer." Enough said.

Buffet

The "sideboard/buffet/hunt board" seems to have been made for just this place. Jeanne Christman, our decorator, found it down in the South Broadway antiques district. It's from Scotland, I know this because when we finally got it home and starting to clean it up, I found the newspaper, now framed and hanging to the left. The Montrose Review, serving Angus and Kincardineshire Scotland, was founded 1831. Dated August 1, 1951, the newspaper was stuck underneath the bottom drawer.

Guests from Scotland often remark how wonderful it is and point out the carvings of Highland Roses and Oak garlands that remind them of home.

The trophy head you see above the sideboard is, I am told, that of a European Stag, not an American deer. It was quite traditional we are told, to have trophy heads in Victorian homes here in the west.

The Family Parlor/Conservatory

This story begins with the 1890 photograph you see beside the Grandfather Clock. Oh, and note the slight floor step-up from the dining Room. It shows the Back or Family Parlor as it originally was. The picture was taken from the Dining Room looking through the gorgeous Moorish Fret doorway between the Back and Front Parlor with its wonderful mantelpiece. Note the south wall with its elegant three-windowed bay. There was a fireplace mantel and hearth on the east wall where the bookcase now stands. Basically, the Back Parlor room you see in the photo was moved to where a sunroom had been located and rebuilt, three-windowed bay and all. This is our Conservatory and bath today. Its roof created the veranda space for the Van Cise Room on the second floor. Oh yes, they moved the floor as well, note the fireplace hearth in the Conservatory under the dresser, hence the slight step-up into our Parlor from the Foyer and Dining Room.

Two larger rooms were built in its place, our Back Parlor, and kitchen.

All in all, I consider the Foyer the most original Room in the mansion, the Dining Room second.

The Dining Room

After studying the 1890 photograph, then measured by the replication of the ceiling art, "replica" chandelier, the Lincrusta wall covering, was made by the Walton Company in England. The room has its original stained glass, window framing, oak paneling down to the quarter-sawn oak flooring and doors. Note the leaded glass windows in the 1890 photo were draped over. No idea why.

Originally there were two "pocket doors" in the room, one from the Foyer and the other from the Back Parlor. When the mansion was converted to an apartment house, the doorway from the Back Parlor was closed and walled over, as the first floor was divided into two units. The door from the Parlor was taken out of the "pocket," hinged and became the front door to Apartment #1.

Another story… We had been open just a couple of years. One evening I was closing the house down when I noticed a guest in the Dining Room, his head down, eyes closed softly rubbing the wood trim beside the Dining Room Door. At first I didn't think to disturb him, but stopped, turned and respectfully, asked if there was any way I could help him. He stopped rubbing the wood trim and turned to me smiled and said, "The wood feels good." He had been rubbing his hand over a section of trim that had an old cigarette burn in it. I started to apologize that the wood probably needed to be cleaned. He stopped me and softly said, "No you didn't understand what I said, the wood in this house feels good. It feels good." Another lesson learned.

The Conservatory

The guest room we call the "Conservatory" has an interesting history. When the house was built, the original doorway we see was the entrance to a conservatory, or sunroom but considering its grand entrance, it was more than just an iron and glass hothouse. More of what was called a "Summerhouse" room where the family could enjoy flowers, plants, and sunshine all year long.

I have mentioned how the original home changed drastically since when it was converted into a seven-unit apartment house in 1918-1920. A few changes occurred when it became an office building in 1973-1974. Of course, many changes were made to make the Castle Marne what you see today.

The Holland Suite

The Holland Suite was named for Lyle Holland, owner of the mansion from 1938 until his death in 1972. He lived in the unit on the 1st floor, south side.

The first bedroom originally was the kitchen for the mansion; the hallway was the Butler's Pantry. The archway in the Dining Room was constructed when the mansion was converted to apartments after the World War I. The second bedroom at the rear of the building was constructed at the same time. The unit was converted to office space in 1973-1974. We walled in the archway during our restoration in 1988-1989 to create an on site manager's quarters. My wife Diane and I lived there until 2004 when we moved into the Carriage House, and the Holland Suite was created as our 10th room. Note the thickness of the wall between the two bedrooms; it is the original 1889 back wall of the mansion.

CHAPTER THIRTEEN

The Second Floor Tour

Peacock Window ❖ Foxy Mirror ❖ Good Night

Peacock Window

The round crystal leaded glass Peacock Window has been the hallmark of the mansion since it was built in 1889. I had been noticing and wondering about the window since we first saw the building.

Shortly after we closed the sale, I noticed that the window was bowing out along the bottom. I decided it was time to have someone come out and tell me if I should be concerned about it, so I went to the Yellow Pages, do you remember them? I turned to Stained Glass

Window Repairs. There was quite a list of names. As I was scrolling down the list, my finger stopped and my eye was drawn to Watkins Stained Glass Studio. A little voice said to call this one. I called and described my situation and set an appointment to have the window looked at.

When the gentleman arrived, he introduced himself as Phil Watkins, took one look up at the window, and he said, "My great grandfather Clarence made that window." I could hardly speak, the little voice was right. I asked him about the bowing out, he said with a smile, "When you get to be 100 years old, you will probably bow out a bit too, and not to worry." He went on to tell me more about the window and that his great grandfather had lived just around the corner on Vine Street. He said the window is unique; there is not another window like it in the city. Clarence designed it just for this building.

The Peacock

Many Denver mansions have a Peacock Window, but they are an actual representation of the bird itself. Ours is a surrealistic representation of a peacock with its tail feathers spread. Note the elongated crystal beveled glass panels around the window's edge as the feathers. Next you see the colored roundels representing the eyes in the outstretched

tail feathers. In the center of the window, note the head, eyes, beak, wings, body and even the feathered topknot on its head. You may have to use your imagination a bit, but it's all there. Phil told me all the glass was made in Belgium, and has not been available since before World War I. He also told me the pink and gold shades of color were a result of actual gold being fused into the glass when it was being made.

The Rock

You will notice a rock about the size of a potato lying on the windowsill to the left. Like most everything else around here, there is a story behind it.

Before we started construction, we put ¼-inch plexiglass on both the inside and outside of the window to protect it during reconstruction. To my knowledge, there had not been any protection on the window before. About 10 years later, a guest had finished breakfast and was walking around the house to the parking lot. He rushed back in and said, "Come with me, you have to see what has happened." Outside, scattered on the sidewalk and lawn was the shattered plexiglass that had been covering the window. I ran back into the house and up the stairs to see the rock and pieces of the window between the interior plexiglass and the window. The rock had shattered the exterior plexiglass and done a small amount of damage to the window itself, I was stunned, and realized I had to call Phil Watkins. When he arrived, he said there had been very little structural damage done. I said I had fit the pieces back in place and secured them with scotch tape. He explained to me that to do any other repairs, the window would have to be removed, taken to his studio and completely rebuilt and that there was over a four-year waiting list before he could start the restoration. He assured me the window was not going to fall apart and it will see many years of use.

To this day we have no idea who did this or why they did it. If you look carefully, you can see the repairs. I replaced the exterior plexiglass with bullet proof Lexan plastic.

Fleur-de-lis

About 15 years after our opening, I realized that the plaster cast Fleur-de-lis had originally been gold-gilded, not just painted the same color as the walls. A bunch of us spent one entire summer, using tiny paintbrushes, painting every one of the new 396 Fleur-de-lis, as well as every one of the original Foyer wall castings that had not been damaged. They looked so good, I set about to gild the pressed-plaster decorations on the ceiling and frieze of the Foyer. As I learned, pressed-plaster style of decorating was sometimes used as a substitute for hand-painted ceiling art. Plaster would be troweled on the ceiling or frieze, when a carved wooden die was pressed into the plaster as it set. The pattern would then be replicated all around the frieze or ceiling creating an amazing two-dimensional effect. Looking at the 1890 photo in the Foyer, you will notice the pressed plaster replaced the original hand-painted ceiling and frieze, probably around the turn-of-the-century.

Mirror

The Pier Mirror is also known as a Trumeau or Petticoat Mirror, because women could examine themselves in the long mirror to see if their petticoats were showing. Often this was called a diamond dust mirror, because if you shine a light on the glass you will see what appears to be a dusty diamond like reflection, as if there was actual diamond dust coating the back of the mirror. There really are no diamond dust mirrors. Actually this is a process whereby the original silver/mercury coating goes through a process known as foxing. Heat, light, and age will cause the reflective coating to break down, effecting a change in the reflection of light back to our eyes; but I still like the diamond dust story. The mirror is not original to the mansion, we purchased it at auction.

Stairway Post

Note the stairway newel post with the beehive-looking cap at the second floor landing. The ornamentation had been stolen or broken before we arrived. All during the reconstruction we were up and down the stairs, thinking we need to have another cap made, as the inside was hollow and full of trash. We had often talked about having a time capsule, maybe a cornerstone sort of thing, perhaps buried in the yard. But we never seemed to get around to it.

One day as I was going past the topless newel post, it suddenly occurred to me here was our time capsule right under our noses all the time. We carefully removed the beehive cap from another newel post and had a duplicate made for the top of our time capsule, with a small brass plaque saying "Castle Marne August 1st, 1989."

A day before we opened for business, the time capsule was filled with newspapers of the day, a complete set of working plans, blueprints, cards wishing the family good luck, photos of the construction, a set of 1989 coins, and assorted mementos. All were sealed inside. We haven't decided when to open it.

The Clock

The antique wall clock was the first old clock I bought. I bought it when I was about 16 years old. It got me started collecting clocks. I now have at least 40 of all sorts, shapes, and sizes. Note the hands are set at eleven minutes past eleven. It is traditional that a clock not running, should have its hands set at that time. This is to commemorate the Armistice, which was signed November 11, 1917 at eleven o'clock a.m. This led to the Treaty of Versailles, signed June 28, 1918, officially ending WWI.

Fixtures

The hall light fixture on the landing is the only light fixture that was here that we could use. It was the Foyer chandelier when we bought the castle.

The hall ceiling light fixtures are reproductions, but they look the period and add a great deal to the overall warmth of our inn.

Doors

All of the wooden panel doors are original to the mansion, and were in use on the first, second, and third floors. The City Building Inspectors first said we would have to get rid of the wood doors, as they would not meet the one-hour fire code. After much discussion, they decided that using the original wood panel doors on the first and second floors could pass code, but that new fire-rated doors must be used on the third floor. I quickly agreed.

The transoms above the doors were originally glass windows that opened out into the hall to facilitate movement of air. Current fire code required the glass be replaced by one-hour rated sheetrock or wire-reinforced safety glass. I chose the sheetrock.

The Presidential Suite

The Presidential Suite is our premier offering. I picked the name because in my travels, really classy places always had a Presidential Suite. The photograph in the room is one of the original pictures I found at the Denver Public Library, showing the owners' quarters as they were back in 1890. The fireplace mantel was stolen, but we were able to build another from the picture. Some day we hope to have the ceiling repainted to match the original.

Note the room blueprint-like drawing on top of the mantel. It was designed for us by a Japanese interior decorator who visits us every year or so. The small pictures tucked around the mirror are Daguerreotypes and are very old, dating back to the 1830s.

The picture to the left of the mantel is special. My mother always wanted to go to Paris, and before she died, she was able to go. She asked if she could bring me back something. I thought a bit and said, "I would like an original signed painting of somewhere special in Paris." She brought back this painting of a scene in the Montmartre.

To the left of the painting you see a small dresser, which was given to us by a friend shortly before she died. I don't know if it was a child's toy or perhaps a furniture salesman's sample.

We searched far and wide for the dresser like the one you see in the picture, it's called a "Gentleman's Hat Box" dresser. When you open the small door you will find a space designed so the gentleman of the house could store his tall silk hat out of the dusty air.

The framing and wall you see behind the bed was not original, but added after it became an apartment house, giving access from the front room into the adjoining rooms of the unit. We closed it off as it had been originally intended.

The black and white photograph on the west wall was taken in 1890. The bed was a fancy standard size brass bed, with unusual brass and lace ornamental panels. Our Presidential Suite would have a king-size bed that looked like that, but what about the fancy brass and lace at the head of the bed? I took the photo to bed stores all over town and asked if they knew where I could get a new king size bed that looked like the photo. They all said no, they didn't, but if I did find one to let them know as they would certainly like to add it to their inventory. Undaunted, I bought an old beat up brass bed frame, took it apart and made the swing arms, then sewed the lace, bolted them on, and finished off with a pair of lamp finials to look like the originals. It's not a bad job, eh?

We started to strip paint from all the woodwork in the room. The tower alcove and wood trim is truly a delight to look at, but took an ungodly amount of work to strip the paint and refinish the wood.

A note on paint stripping is necessary here. We tried chemical strippers, but with very little success; there were over thirty coats of paint on the woodwork. I bought three electric heat guns at Home Depot but they lasted only a few days. I finally bought three professional-grade heat guns. They cost us an arm and a leg, but boy did they do the job. They operate at two speeds settings; 500 degrees or 1,000 degrees. After learning how to not burn the wood or ourselves, we could effectively remove the layers of paint with the heat guns, putty knives, and steel wool. We noticed that after a few hours of paint removal, we would feel a bit lightheaded, but didn't think anything of it. After a good night's sleep we forgot about it. It didn't occur to us that using the heat guns released chemical vapors as the lead paint softened. We were in too big a hurry to finish and open for business so we just didn't think about the risk of lead poisoning.

Van Cise Room

There are no original photos, but we believe the Van Cise Room originally was the second floor Family Parlor, with the wonderful fireplace and mantel, and the three-bay windows enhancing the aura of the room. The present doorway into the bathroom was not there in the beginning. Being the only bathroom for the mansion, it was accessed by its door from the hall.

Today the Van Cise Room is probably our favorite room, with its private balcony, umbrella table and hot tub, original bathroom, original mantel and woodwork, albeit painted as we ran out of time to strip the paint.

This is a funny story. The fireplace opening was bricked up, and I wondered why. One day I sat down on the floor in front it with my legs spread apart, with a small sledgehammer I began to carefully knock out the bricks. When I had removed most all the bricks, I could see a beautiful cast iron firebox liner, which would scrub up nicely. I reached in to check the damper, which fell open and a chimney full of ash and soot came pouring down, filling the firebox and into my lap and all over my face and head. It took all day to clean me as well as the room.

The original bathroom served the family with a stool, marble top sink and cast iron claw footed bathtub. In the apartment house days, each unit had its bathroom and kitchen. Many were removed when it became offices. We cut the access door from the Van Cise bedroom to the original bath, making it the Van Cise room's private bath. We were able to save the wall tile and fixtures, but not the floor, which had to be retiled. A funny thing happened when a workman was taking the marble backsplash off of the sink to repair the wall behind. He yelled to me, "Jim come here, you have got to see this." I went up to the Van Cise bathroom, and he showed me what he had discovered. On the back of the marble, two names had been written in pencil, Geo Rice and H.A. Russell, dated February, 1890. They must have been the plumbers who were working on the bathroom and left us a note. It was wonderful, but now looking back, not an unprepared for surprise.

About 15 years later, after an article was written about us in a travel magazine, in which I mentioned this story, a woman from Georgia, called me to say that that Geo Rice was her great grandfather. Small world isn't it?

Raymond Room

When the residence was converted into a seven-unit apartment house in 1919, an addition was added on the back of the building, which became part of our present first floor Holland Suite, and second floor Raymond Room balcony. While it is our smallest room, the large balcony with its private hot tub and umbrella table, make it an especially popular room.

The Lang Room

The Lang Room was named for William Lang, the famous architect of our mansion. A copy of the only known photograph of Mr. Lang is hanging on the wall in the room. The high four-poster bed with steps to climb into bed is a favorite, but don't worry; no one has ever fallen out of bed.

The bronze bust in the first floor Parlor was carved from this picture.

CHAPTER FOURTEEN

The Third Floor Tour
Photographs ✣ Butterflies ✣ Heirlooms

Ballroom

Originally, the third floor of the mansion was the Ballroom. Today you have to sort of use your imagination to see a large open room with two elaborate fireplaces furnishing warmth, an 18-foot cathedral ceiling, and a beautiful oak dance floor. The present third floor Parlor, Melissa's Room, Tower Room, and John Mason Room represent the original space. Colonel Platt's Room space was added in the 1920s.

The 1890 photo of the front exterior of the mansion shows us there was an open-air balcony on the third floor front, which opened off of the Ballroom. It allowed occupants to step out of the Ballroom for a breath of fresh air, or a smoke. Note the two windowless openings, windows and casings were installed and interior walls removed when the Ballroom became apartments.

The owners were wealthy and moved comfortably in Denver's high society where dances and other social functions were the order of the day. They would occasionally hire a troop of players to entertain the neighborhood children with *Punch and Judy* shows and other entertainment, perhaps for birthday parties. Prior to a major social event, they might have a trunk show for neighborhood women to show the latest fashions, put on by downtown merchants and department stores.

Butterflies

Hanging on the wall starting down the hall on your left, is a framed *Rocky Mountain Newspaper* article dated May 17, 1896, describing the "LIFE OF THE BUTTERFLY and the world class moth and butterfly collection belonging to Mr. John T. Mason, the new owner of 1572 Race Street." The article went on praising his famous collection, which he was working on in the third floor of the mansion when the reporter interviewed him. The smaller framed article below LIFE OF THE

BUTTERFLY, describes Jack Mason donating his collection to the Colorado Museum of Natural History, in 1918.

We were open maybe a year and I was learning about John Mason, the third owner of the mansion and a founder of the Colorado Museum of Natural History, (now the Denver Museum of Nature and Science). I have already referenced him and his famous moth and butterfly collection, which he donated to the museum in 1918 when he moved to California. It is no longer on display, but now a research collection not accessible to the public.

We had gotten to know some people in the Zoology department at the museum, and an idea occurred to me. We had a lot of wall space up on the third floor, and wouldn't it be grand if the museum would let us borrow a few of Mr. Mason's display cases to decorate the third floor.

From owner John Mason's memorial moth and butterfly collection. Displayed on the third floor.

After all, we had restored his mansion and would hang them where he worked on them; but they said, "No." They said "no" because the collection is uninsurable, fragile, etc. But they did offer a solution to my request. If we were to furnish wooden display cases made to their specifications, they would prepare and mount a display collection for us as a memorial to Mr. Mason. They gave us specifications for the butterfly cases.

My son-in-law's father was a cabinet maker by trade so he and Louie made eight cases, which I took to the museum. They mounted and annotated the collection now on display on our third floor. None of the moths or butterflies are from Mr. Mason's original collection.

The two cases in the Mason Room, titled "Butterflies of Colorado" are especially interesting. We are told that Colorado has more species of moths and butterflies than any other state. Our museum friends assigned a young Zoology department volunteer to go up into the foothills west of Denver with his butterfly net, and catch as many varieties as he could. We were told that there are probably more butterfly species up in what is known as North Turkey Creek Canyon including Tiny Town, than anywhere else in the state. The resulting two cases are amazing.

Mason Room

Beside the door inside the Mason Room you see two photos, John T. Mason and his second wife Dora Porter Mason.

Hallway Photographs

As you walk down the hall, note the wonderful old photographs. We had been open about a year, when the doorbell rang and there stood a young man with a large bag full of framed photos of early Denver. He told me they were left over from a photo shoot he had been working on, and would I like to buy them. I am not certain, but I think I paid him $100. I hope they weren't stolen goods.

I especially like two views of The Mizpah (Welcome) Arch in front of Union Station at the foot of 17th Street. It was built in 1906 and torn down in 1931, because it was considered a traffic hazard. Of course Buffalo Bill's Farewell Salute in 1907 is special, and the photos of 1880s Larimer Street are wonderful. All of them are unique reminders of Denver's glory days.

Located around the corner to the right of the guest computer is a large map of early Denver. The map was printed in 1888, before the State Capitol was built, and the map shows it facing the wrong way.

To the right of the map you will see a photograph of the Continental Paper Products Company factory taken in the 1930s. This is a photograph of Colonel Platt's paper mill, which became the paper box company my father managed, and where I worked summers during high school, and for six or seven years (as an outside sales representative) after I graduated from college.

Colonel Platt's Room

At the end of the hall you will find what we call Colonel Platt's Room. When we opened for business, we named it the East View Room, as it has a wonderful view of East Denver High School. Several years later, I stumbled on the history of Colonel Platt, who lived in the mansion from 1892 to 1894. It was then I began to realize how much of my family's life was intertwined with his life and times. It is appropriate we renamed the room for him. His picture is on the wall by the bed.

The outdoor two-person hot tub is a favorite as it very private and just right for skinny dipping.

Melissa's Room

In the early 1920s, when the mansion was remodeled into a seven-unit apartment house, the Ballroom and third floor became three small apartments, each with private bath, kitchen, and outside balcony.

One day a couple of years after we opened, a woman came to our door saying that she had lived in an apartment here in the late 1960s, and could she look around? We went up to the third floor to see that her apartment was located on the front of the house where Melissa's Room is now. At the landing as you climb up the wonderful formal stairway, you pass beneath three original windows which face north, at the top of the stairs. Trust me on this, I couldn't make it up. She told me her apartment was very small, and she remembers sitting on the toilet in her bathroom looking out of the westernmost of the three windows down onto 16th Avenue, three floors below. Her bathroom, I realized, was built over the stairway landing, and you might even have had to duck your head to avoid the plumbing pipes when climbing up the stairs.

Melissa's Room is named for my daughter and business partner. The dresser and chair were hers when she was growing up. In 1919 the left-hand window was removed and a doorway was made to access a balcony built above the second floor veranda. We replaced the door with a window so that it looks like it did back in 1890.

The Tower Room

The Tower Room is a comfortable room that accommodates a larger family. Its private bath is just five steps across the hall; not shared with anyone.

We bought the armoire at an auction house. I was told that I had to pick it up the next morning, as they didn't deliver. I arrived back the next morning with a friend's small pick-up truck. It wouldn't fit. The auctioneer told me it was called a "wagon-bed armoire," meaning it came apart in pieces that would fit in the bed of a covered wagon. Made with no screws or nails, only wood pegs, we easily took it apart and slid it into the truck bed with room to spare. We put it back together just as easily up in the Tower Room.

Another fun story! The fireplace mantelpiece was stolen when the house was empty, and there was just a bare space where it once stood.

I belonged to a neighborhood civic organization named Colfax On The Hill (COTH). The vacant Clarko Hotel building at the corner of Colfax and Clarkson had been owned by the city who had taken it over for unpaid taxes. They gave it to COTH for a dollar, and they were ready to tear the building down. It had long been a rundown abandoned eyesore. Among the tenants had been a dirty book store, a porn theater, and the famous San Francisco Topless Shoe Shine Parlor. I was able to get into the empty building to see if there was anything salvageable. Upon the second floor, in a back room, was an old beat-up fireplace mantel. I measured, and it was just about the size of the mantel that had been stolen from our castle. The problem remained as to how to get it back to our Castle Marne, as they were to begin razing the building the next morning. My friend with the pick-up had moved, so my son Riley and I decided to carry it home. It was heavy and awkward to move, but we finally got it down the stairs, and began to lug it up Colfax. We attracted a lot of attention when a newspaper photographer happened along and took our picture. Soon after that a very nice fellow in a pick-up truck stopped and offered to take us and the mantel home. Louie found fleur-de-lis tiles in a second hand store. It looks like it belongs there, except for the exterior stone exposed above it. I wanted to drywall it in so the stone didn't show, but I was overruled. We filled the top with books, it looks great.

On the fireplace mantel to the left you see a photo of Dora Porter and her younger sister Laurene. On the right, a 1896 photo of Dora Porter as the Queen of "The Festival of Mountain and Plain." On the desk, you see a photo of my mother-in-law Dorothea O'Leary, at age 18.

The Shelves at the Stair Landing

From the left are two old tin horns, photos of my mother Helen and my father Edwin, Melissa's little tea set, my old Chinese Checkers board, some old tintypes, and my old microscope. I made the Noah's Ark and animals, two rocking horses, and a sailboat for Melissa and Riley when they were kids. The two round framed needlepoint pictures were stitched by my mother. My old baseball mitt, a pair of lawn game rackets made from cow udders, a pair of sad iron bookends, and an assortment of books pretty well fill out the shelves.

My mother was quite a book collector, and the books on the landing and on the Tower Room mantel were hers.

CHAPTER FIFTEEN

The Carriage House

Horses ✤ Studios ✤ Home

In 1974, Louise Dice bought the Marne Apartments and the Carriage House from the Holland family for $130,000. When Louise and Dick Dice first saw the carriage house it was a mess, it had been used as a garage and was filled with abandoned equipment. There was an old cement mixer and fifty years of assorted junk.

The Carriage House and three parking spaces became a separate legal entity, no longer part of 1572 Race Street, now 2020 East 16th Avenue.

In 1976, after an unsuccessful attempt to convert the property into condominiums, Louise hired two enthusiastic young men, Paul Huffman a registered architect, and Brooks Bond to renovate the 2,000 square feet Carriage House into a beautifully appointed studio. In the Home World section of the March 19, 1977, issue of the Denver Post, the headline declares, "Carriage House Regains Look of Former Elegance."

The Carriage House was built of the same lava stone as the mansion. It originally contained stables for four horses, a hayloft, and quarters for two grooms, located on the second floor. Huffman and Bond encountered many challenges during renovation. The foundation was badly settled and the exterior walls were pushed out of line. The original carriage door had to be moved slightly and a new entrance built. With much creative expertise, the two men completed the project. Inspired by a detail in the original wood design, Bond created the stained glass window beside the front door entrance. This motif is carried on to the paneling of the staircase and to the clerestory windows of the eastern office on the ground floor. The oak Foyer was made by tearing out part of the second floor. The brick and rough-cut rafters are sandblasted beams from the original carriage house.

Graphic designer, Lee Reedy, purchased the Carriage House from Louise Dice in 1978 and operated his highly successful graphic arts

The Carriage House at The Marne,
by artist Roger Curley, 1984.

studio there. Lee Reedy and his wife Bonnie operated their graphic arts business in the building until 1984. When they moved into new quarters at 1572 Williams Street, they continued to rent the Carriage House to designer David Robison and some of his associates.

In 1984, the carriage house was occupied by a group of creative associates: David Robison of Robison Advertising Design, Roger Curley of the Roger Curley Studio, John Bergner of Vis-à-vis Phototypesetting, and Christine Patton of C.C. Images.

In 1997, I received a call from Lee asking if I wanted to buy the Carriage House. After some thought, soul searching, and counting our pennies, I said yes. I called Jim Lampman, our financial advisor, who had moved to Seattle, asking him to help me put together a financial package. He agreed and we were on our way. On January 12, 1998, Diane and I signed the papers and were owners of the Carriage House, paying $213,840. We refinanced again in 2003 to remodel it into our living quarters.

PART THREE

The Bed & Breakfast

CHAPTER SIXTEEN

The Inn

World Travelers ✤ Newlyweds ✤ Afternoon Tea

We Got Elegance

Recently Diane and I attended a performance of "Hello Dolly" at the Lakewood Colorado Community Theater. We had seen the show before, but this time it was different, very different. The 1964 Broadway musical with lyrics by Jerry Herman was based on a 1938 Thornton Wilder farce called, *The Merchant of Yonkers*. In the musical, Horace Vandergilt's two clerks, Cornelius and Barnaby, along with his two nieces, Irene and Minnie, are singing and dancing on New York's Second Avenue: "*We got elegance. If you ain't got elegance, you can never ever carry it off.*"

We got elegance. Suddenly those words had new meaning! They were singing about me, my family, and our Castle Marne. Boy, do we have elegance!

Castle Marne Bed & Breakfast has been a family-owned, historic inn since 1989. Located in the heart of Denver's City Park and Capitol Hill neighborhoods, it features ten beautiful rooms decorated in the Victorian style. Castle Marne is a unique wedding venue and offers vintage teas, catered candlelight dinners, and castle-made breakfasts every morning for guests from around the world. Our first brochure introducing us to the world quoted Alfred Lord Tennyson, "Splendor Falls From Castle Walls."

Not long ago Diane and I were having dinner with some old high school friends, when I was asked (a bit tongue in cheek), how many breakfasts I have served over the last 28 years? I replied that I hadn't counted and couldn't imagine. An engineer friend got out a pen, opened a fresh paper napkin and began to figure it out. Finally, after a lot of scribbling and high mathematic calculations, he announced that since we opened Castle Marne, I had served approximately 148,592 breakfasts. Based on his degree in mathematics he would guarantee it, and who am I to argue.

From the day I first saw the building that would become the Castle Marne, I began to realize that a unique symbiotic relationship existed between us. A couple of years after we had opened, I read a book called *The Celestine Prophecies*, written by James Redfield. His book and its philosophy set me on the path to a better understanding about my developing rapport with that big old stone building with the round window.

Throughout the process of writing this book, I often mused about how it all related, but then as Shakespeare said, "Thereby hangs a tale."

This set me to thinking about a comment a guest recently made to us. He said he stayed with us twenty-six years ago, and did we remember him, he certainly remembered and recognized us. His name sort of rang a bell, but I didn't remember his face. Considering the number of breakfasts I have served, plus a lot of guests who didn't eat or missed breakfast,   maybe a quarter of a million folks have passed through our doors. WOW!

We began to realize that the Castle Marne has an unusual capacity of impressing and expressing our image, experience, spirit, presence, or whatever you could call it on those who have stayed with us over the years. Positive remembrances of us for many and varied reasons continue to enhance our image. Try that on Hilton.

- *Those who bring sunshine to others cannot keep it from themselves…*Barrie

- *We shall be judged, not by what we might have been, but what we have been…*Sewell

- *When you are sincerely pleased, you are nourished…*Emerson

Weddings

I suppose that over the years, we have performed more than a hundred weddings here at The Castle. Melissa, Louie, and grandson Louie J., and I are all licensed wedding officiates. Our specialty is small weddings and elopements, but we have done ceremonies and receptions for up to 60 people. While all weddings are special, a few stand out in my memory.

Log Home Show Weddin'

One morning, as I was preparing breakfast, the phone rang and a man asked if we did "weddin's." I said, "Yes we do, and when were you planning to be married?" He replied, "Today. Me and my girlfriend are drivin' up from Oklahoma and are comin' to Denver for the Log Home Show. Last night we decided to get married."

I chuckled to myself and asked where they were staying?

"We spent last night here in Lamar and are comin' to Denver today. Could you marry us?"

I gathered my composure and asked what time they thought they would be here. I told him that they needed to stop at a County Court House on the way and buy a wedding license. He replied they would probably be here around two o'clock and needed directions.

I told the story to Melissa when she came in, she said she would prepare a ceremony just in case they showed up. Well, to make a long story short, at about two o'clock they pulled up in front driving an old well-worn pick-up truck. They got out and came in, gave me their wedding license, a bottle of champagne to celebrate with and asked when could we start?

I got on my black robe, Melissa put on wedding music and I performed the ceremony. We signed the license, and had a glass of champagne. They thanked us, got in their truck and were off to the Log Home Show. They were a very nice couple. We never saw them again.

Engagement and Suit of Armor

I got a call from a young man who told me that he wanted to propose to his girlfriend in our castle, with period costumes and all the rest. We talked a bit and he said they were history buffs, into Knights and Princesses. He wanted to come by to discuss it further. He had it all planned. His Princess would be awaiting her Knight standing on our Presidential Suite balcony in full period princess garb. He would arrive on horse-back, dressed in a full suit of armor, dismount and then, down on one knee, he would propose to her. Of course, all of this would be a surprise to her. They would then spend the night with us after a private dinner in our Dining Room. How could we pass on this one?

Well, the day arrived and she checked in alone. He had told her he had a surprise for her and would be along a bit later. She was completely unaware of what was coming. We showed her up to the room where there was a complete princess costume, which he had rented and brought by earlier that day. It was laying out on the bed ready to put on. We told her she was to get dressed and wait out on the balcony and not to ask any questions. She told us her boyfriend thought up some crazy things, but this may be the topper. She decided she would go along with it. I was then supposed to run down the block to the IHOP parking lot where her boyfriend would be waiting, dressed in a full suit of armor astride a horse. The plan was he would gallop down Race Street, up onto our sidewalk, alight, kneel, and propose.

Well, things didn't work out as planned. The man who was to bring the horse didn't show up. There he was, dressed in his armor all ready, thinking "my kingdom for a horse!"

He had asked a friend to be there to help him get ready. He had driven his Ford Mustang convertible. The groom took one look at the car, and not to be denied, told his friend to put down the top. He would stand in the back seat of the mustang and be driven down Race Street to the Castle where he would dismount his mustang, walk up our sidewalk just as planned, and propose to his waiting princess. Well, he did and she said, yes.

That's quite a story but there's more. They came down for dinner, he in a regular suit, not of armor, she in a beautiful dress. They were shown into the Dining Room. As usual, we set the places across from each other at the middle of the table. He looked at the table and asked if we could reset the places, one at each end of the table, as a Knight and his Princess would have been served in medieval times. They stepped out into the Parlor and we reset the table. They came back in and were seated at the ends of the table twelve-feet away from each other. I proceeded to serve the first course and quietly left the room for them to enjoy their candlelight dinner. When I came back in to pick up the plates, they rather sheepishly asked if we would reset the table again. They couldn't imagine how people actually enjoyed that sort of dining arrangement.

They came back later and were married in a tuxedo and a wedding gown. They have been back several times to celebrate their anniversary.

Wiccan Wedding

We got a call from a couple who asked if we would perform a Wiccan wedding. We said we hadn't done one before, but come over and we can talk about it. We read up on Wiccan weddings and were very interested to discuss it when they arrived. They were in their mid-forties. He was at least six-feet, three-inches tall and she was nearly six-feet tall. There would be only the two of them in the wedding party.

They had consulted with a shaman to determine the day and time for the wedding. It was to be on Halloween. They described the ceremony in detail and it was going to be very special. The day arrived and the time was to be 7:00 p.m. They checked in early and were staying in the Presidential Suite.

The groom and I were waiting at the foot of the stairs a bit before 7:00 p.m. He was wearing a beautiful long blue velvet robe with a hood. A sword in a scabbard was on a leather belt at his side. At the appointed time she came down the stairs from the second floor, stopping on the landing, where she motioned for him to join her. She was wearing a black velvet robe with a hood. He went up the stairs to the landing, where he drew his sword and knelt down as he presented it to her. She took the sword, and after some words were exchanged, he removed his hood and she touched the blade of the sword on each of his shoulders. She had dubbed, or had chosen him, for her own. He stood up, took the sword, put it back in the scabbard and they came down the stairs together into the Parlor where I was waiting. She then removed her hood. The ceremony was wonderful. First was a call to the gods to watch over and bless the couple, then, vows and rings were exchanged. A beautiful binding ceremony was preformed where a velvet cord was carefully and symbolically bound around their wrists. These were the ties that would bind them together for eternity.

Then they "jumped the broom." Jumping of the broom is an ancient Celtic rite used to symbolize fertility and prosperity of the couple. It signifies their entrance into a new life and their creation of a new family by symbolically sweeping away their former single lives, former problems and concerns. After jumping over the broom, they would enter a new adventure as wife and husband. They brought a special broom for the ceremony. It is said the higher the broom is held, the more fertile the marriage will be. After the appropriate words were said, they asked that the broom lay flat on the floor and they would simply step over it. Final prayers were said, I declared them husband and wife, they kissed, and the wedding was over. This was one of the most meaningful ceremonies I was ever privileged to perform.

Tall and Short of It

We were approached by a gentleman who worked at Martin Marietta in Littleton. He had fallen in love with a rocket engineer in Silicon Valley. He told us they had searched and searched, deciding the Castle Marne was the perfect place to have their wedding, so it was booked and the day was set. Melissa began planning the wedding, working closely with the bride by email and telephone; writing the ceremony to suit their wishes, selecting the music, planning the reception, ordering flowers and arranging for the photographer. She took charge of all the details. The bride was still in California and would not arrive until the day of the wedding. Both families would be represented, all together about 25 persons. There was no scrimping on anything. It was going to be the perfect wedding.

The groom was middle-aged, about six-feet tall and rather shy. We had never seen the bride. The day of the wedding arrived and guests were assembling. We still had not seen the bride. I had my black marrying robe on, standing in the front Parlor with the Groom and Best Man, waiting. The music started, the guests rose to watch the Maid of Honor come down the stairs and finally, the Bride started down the stairs. She was dressed in a beautiful veiled gown with a long train. She was barely three-feet tall! She was escorted in and stood by her husband-to-be. I started the ceremony, trying to look into each face as I spoke, my head bobbing up and down, up and down. I just couldn't do it. I stopped the ceremony, explained my difficulty, and asked if we could stand the bride on a box or something. They all smiled and agreed that it would be a good idea. Melissa rushed into the kitchen and came out with a green plastic dairy case, covered it with a large decorated cloth. The Groom lifted his Bride up and the ceremony began again. We all agreed it was one of the finest weddings we had ever done at the Castle.

Travel Associations

On August 1st, 1989, after a year of raising the money, renovating and restoring the building, we set about the business of operating our bed and breakfast.

High on the list was marketing, promoting and advertising ourselves as the newest B&B in Denver. Other B&Bs, including, *Victoria Oaks,* across the street, the *Queen Anne Inn,* and *The Merritt House* were very helpful with advice to get us off on the right foot. Local travel writers, especially Doris and Gary Kennedy, assisted us with articles and pictures.

"Thoughts of coziness and comfort come to mind when describing Castle Marne, a recently opened neighborhood B&B located at 1572 Race Street. Elegant yet comfortable, is how its 'caretakers,' the James Peiker family, describe it." *LIFE on Capitol Hill* (October 20, 1989)

When we opened, the Internet didn't exist and marketing was a whole different animal. The building was known as the Raymond House and The Marne. The Raymond House didn't mean much to us so we decided to be The Marne. *The Yellow Pages* advertising was a powerful tool and to be at the top of the listing was important, so we rather jokingly added Castle to our name, moving us to the top of the list. After all, we did look like a castle.

We were fortunate to have a lot of positive press from local newspapers and travel magazines, telling the world about a new B&B in Denver. Throughout the Rocky Mountain West, Bed and Breakfasts were a new concept in the lodging industry. What we really needed was the recognition and perception as a legitimate lodging alternative.

We were able to get it through memberships in trade associations, both local, regional, national and even worldwide. Trade Associations had regular meetings at inns around their membership area. These were very important, as most of us were new to the industry. Staying at other member's properties and discussing their philosophy, dreams and hopes, gave us meaning and understanding of our industry and how we could relate to each other. We were not competitors; we were friends, all part of something new and exciting.

First we joined the Bed and Breakfast Innkeepers of Colorado (BBIC). It had been organized by Sallie and Welling Clark, who owned the *Holden House B&B* in Colorado Springs. Mainly, it was for home stays and small B&Bs. It was an excellent organization, but it didn't seem to be a good fit for us.

Next, we helped organize the Distinctive Inns of Colorado. It was an association of "25 Exceptional Bed and Breakfast Inns throughout Scenic Colorado." This was a very good fit for us and we made many innkeeper friends all around the state. The organization faded away about six-to-eight years ago.

In the late 1960s, a travel writer named Norman Simpson explored America in a wood-paneled station wagon searching for unique places offering exceptional hospitality with "good honest lodgings, good honest food, and good honest feeling." He wrote the first B&B travel guide based on his criteria, *Country Inns and Back Roads.*

It was through Dot and Ruth Williams, who owned and operated the 25-room *Hearthstone Inn* in Colorado Springs that we became members of the Independent Innkeepers of America (IIA). The IIA was organized by owners of properties in New England, that were featured in Norman Simpson's book. It grew into one of the largest travel associations in the country stretching from coast to coast. Some years later the association changed its name to Select Registry. We have been proud members since 1991.

In 1984, a group of historic lodging establishments gathered together to form The Association of Historic Hotels of the Rocky Mountain West (AHWEST). It would be a lodging association quite unlike any other. Membership would be within the Rocky Mountain Time Zone and all properties must be listed on the National Registry of Historic Buildings.

When we joined in 1991, membership had grown to 19 properties with John Feinberg as Executive Director. A few years later the name was changed to Historic Hotels of the Rockies (HHR). For over 20 years, through HHR membership, we were privileged to visit and experience many of the finest historic lodging venues in the country. While a website still exists, the association no longer functions as an operating entity.

We were members of the American Automobile Association, (AAA) for many years, benefiting from their yearly inspections and exposure, but have not belonged for several years.

The following quotation is from the publishers of *Vogue, GQ, Glamour* and *Conde Nast Traveler.*"

"*Conde Nast Johansens* is the leading reference guide for independent travelers. We've hand-selected the best properties from around the world for inclusion in our collection. With over thirty-five years' experience inspecting and recommending properties throughout the world, our team of dedicated and highly-trained Local Experts inspects each property year-on-year. If we recommend a property, you can trust you'll have an exceptional experience."

Conde Nast Johansens Award

Conde Nast asked us to be their Denver recommended property in 1995. For many years they had been the leader in presenting elegant accommodations to discriminating travelers throughout the world. While it was expensive and we really didn't get a lot of business from our membership, it had a great deal of snob and elitist appeal. We felt we had really hit the big time to be featured in their gorgeous yearly guidebook along with the finest properties in the world.

In early 2004, we were notified the Castle Marne was to be nominated for the 2005 award for MOST OUTSTANDING SMALL INN-NORTH AMERICA. That summer we were notified that our award was to be presented at *The Conde Nast Johansens* Awards Luncheon at The Dorchester, London on November 8, 2004. Diane and I booked our flight and were there to receive our award. It is very difficult to describe the elegance, the setting, the grace, and respect with which the award was presented to us. You can view the award in our Foyer where it is proudly displayed.

Extra Mile Award

I was very proud to be recognized with this award given by the *Denver Convention and Visitors Bureau* at a special meeting on March 27, 2015.

"In recognition of your motivation to go the EXTRA Mile to make exceptional hospitality a way of life in Denver."

Brian Parsons, our Innkeeper, wrote this letter nominating me for the EXTRA Mile Award given each year by the Bureau. "Jim is one of the most dedicated men I've ever met. He has worked tirelessly for over 25 years and has entertained our guests with stories of Denver's past, as well as the Castle's. He has dedicated his life to the restoration of this historic landmark building and to the preservation of Denver's history. Jim is everything that a young innkeeper like myself strives to be. He touches everyone that steps through our doors and welcomes everyone into Castle Marne as anyone would welcome you into their home."

Other Awards

1989   THE COLORADO HISTORICAL SOCIETY

1989   INN BUSINESS REVIEW

1990   DENVER'S UPTOWN ON THE HILL ASSOCIATION

1990   CAPITOL HILL UNITED NEIGHBORHOODS

1991   BED & BREAKFAST INNKEEPERS OF COLORADO ASSN

1992   COLFAX ON THE HILL- CHAIRMAN'S AWARD

1994   AMERICAN BED & BREAKFAST ASSOCIATION

2001   SUNSET MAGAZINE GREAT COOK AWARD

2001-4 ROCKY MOUNTAIN NEWS- PEOPLE'S CHOICE AWARD
        for TOP B&B IN DENVER

CHAPTER SEVENTEEN

The Tales

Fun ✤ Famous ✤ Unforgettable

Tiny Tim

People often ask who my favorite guest was and I tell them this story… Back in 1990, two friends of ours, Thom Wise and Lannie Garrett, opened a small nightclub over on 17th Avenue, called RUBY'S. They brought in noteworthy performers who were, well, past the headliner big spotlight, but still had it. They had been open a few months when I saw Thom and asked him why he didn't have any of his performers stay with us. He said I was too good a friend and he wouldn't risk our friendship. They were generally rude, surly, selfish and not the Castle Marne kind of guest. I didn't ask again. It was two or three months later, he called and said he wanted to reserve a room for a performer coming in a couple of months. I remembered our conversation and asked the name. "I won't tell you," he said, but he will be a great Castle Marne guest. I asked him several other times but he still wouldn't say who it was.

The day finally arrived and we were all anxiously waiting to meet our mystery guest. Another friend in the neighborhood had an old Rolls Royce limousine he said belonged to the Prince of Wales and he was bringing our guest in style. The limo pulled up and Tiny Tim got out. Thom was grinning ear-to-ear as he escorted him into the Marne. He looked just like he did on television. Tiny Tim glanced up at the 1889 National Register historic plaque hanging on the wall behind me, and asked me if I knew the number one musical hit in 1889. Rather startled, I replied I didn't know. He said it was "Down Went McGinty to the Bottom of the Sea." I laughed and told him I remembered my Mother would sing that song to me when I was a little boy. We later realized he had a photographic memory.

We welcomed him and introduced ourselves. He said he was rather tired from traveling and asked me to show him to his room. Back at the front desk we were chatting with Thom and getting over the shock. I heard his voice from the second floor landing, "Excuse me Mr. Pike, could you come up to my room?" He would always call me Mr. Pike.

When I got to his room he was shaking and white as a sheet. He pointed up to a bunch of miller moths flying around the ceiling fan over the bed. "I can't stay here if those are here," he said. I started to explain to him they were harmless and we have them every spring. He interrupted me and with his voice trembling he said, "You don't understand, they will eat my face."

We now know it is a medical condition known as *lepidodteritus,* or fear of moths and butterflies; he was not joking. I quickly took off my shoes and climbed up and stood on the mattress, grabbing each one, I then put them in my pants pocket. Where else would I put them? I got all ten or twelve of them and got down off of the bed. He thanked me and said he would take a nap now, as he had a rehearsal that evening before the first show.

We came to know the drummer in Tiny Tim's pick-up band and he later told us about the first rehearsal. In the back-up band there was a drummer, base, and keyboard. That afternoon, they were waiting at the nightclub for their rehearsal, not knowing what to expect. Tiny Tim arrived, asked their names, thanked them, got his ukulele out of its canvas bag, turned to them and said, "Please give me a C." They looked at each other and finally the keyboard guy hit a C. Tiny Tim strummed his Uke and said, "Thank you, I will see you at the first show". He then turned and walked away. They were stunned.

What kind of a rehearsal was this? They were still wondering what they were supposed to do at the first show. They were ready, but for what? That evening when Tiny Tim came on stage, he bowed, smiled, and waved to the audience. Then he pulled a small blue Spiral note pad out of his pocket and began reading from it. He thanked Thom and Lannie, the taxi driver that brought him to the club, Mr. Pike and the nice folks at the Castle Marne B&B where he was staying; and each band member by name.

He got his ukulele out of the canvas bag, turned to the band and said, "Please give me a C," and he began to sing. The band reacted quickly, picking up on the song he was singing and the show was on the road, as they say. Tiny Tim sang several sets of four songs before breaking for some comments about the weather, the nightclub and the audience before he went back to another set of four songs. He would sing a set of four World War I songs, four June songs, four 30s songs, four World War II songs, four moon songs; well, you get the idea.

During the breaks, Thom or Lannie would welcome the audience and talk about upcoming shows. Each show Tiny Tim would do a fantastic Elvis impersonation, complete with the singing, rolling hips, shakes, and improvisation. It all made for a great evening. Tiny Tim didn't hit all the high falsetto notes he once did, but it made for an amazing night with a remarkable performance. He was a true professional, giving his all to please his audience.

I would like to make a few comments about this talented, very unique and, I believe, misunderstood gentleman. He was the man you saw and heard. He was polite, caring, and empathetic. He wasn't a great musician, but a wonderful entertainer committed to his profession and craft. I have always said there was not a phony bone in his body. He was a showman in every sense of the word.

He showered four-to-five times a day, obsessed with cleanliness. He brushed his teeth many times a day for at least 10 minutes each time, using four different toothbrushes, each with different paste or powder. His skin was soft as a baby's. His shoulder length hair was shiny and luxurious. When I asked him about his countenance and bearing, he commented that what his audience saw first and remembered most was his hair, skin, and teeth. That's what they expected him to look like and he worked very hard to give them his best appearance.

When he arrived at the Castle Marne, his luggage consisted of a canvas barrel bag and his ukulele in a canvas satchel. He always wore a light blue Dinner Jacket with dark blue piping, a plaid lumberjack shirt, blue jeans, and canvas shoes. He traveled with one change of clothes.

A day after his arrival, a FedEx driver delivered a rather heavy box for him. We took it up to his room. Several days later, he brought the box down and opened it for us to see. It contained some old sheet music and several dozen old 78 rpm phonograph records. He asked if we would like to have the whole box. He had been collecting the stuff as he traveled, and it seemed to him we were the kind of people who would appreciate and enjoy this gift from him. When we play those

Our favorite guest, Tiny Tim, tip-toeing through the tulips.

records on our 1915 wind-up Victrola, especially "Tip Toe Through The Tulips," our thoughts are of him.

He would be home after his last show, and be up around 10:30 in the morning, not eating with our other guests. He wasn't rude, but shy and somewhat introverted, always polite and soft-spoken. Around noon, he would ask me to call a taxi for him. Most every afternoon he would go to senior citizen homes to perform, walking in unannounced to entertain them and brighten their day. I suspect not many knew this side of the man.

Born on April 12, 1932, as Herbert Buckingham Khaury, Tiny Tim was raised in the Washington Heights section of New York City. He told us his first job was as a bicycle courier on Wall Street delivering securities. Eventually adopting the name Tiny Tim from the Charles Dickens character, he began performing in clubs in the busy Greenwich Village music scene. He also played at talent shows and parties. His parents tried to dissuade him from pursuing a career in music, but he was committed. An appearance in the 1968 movie, You Are What You Eat, led to getting booked on *Rowan and Martin's Laugh-In*, a hugely popular television variety show. His high-pitched falsetto voice, ukulele playing, and unusual appearance fascinated Dan Rowan. Tiny Tim was an instant novelty hit. He was over six-feet tall and wore his dark, curly, hair to his shoulders. He appeared several more times on *Laugh-In* and became a regular on Johnny Carson's *Tonight Show*. He had a hit with his remake of the old standard song, "Tip-Toe Through The Tulips With Me." His wedding to fiancée, Miss Vicki, on *The Tonight Show,* drew the most viewers in the show's history.

Tiny Tim and Miss Vicki divorced after eight years and one child, a daughter named Victoria Tulip. He would marry two more times. He suffered a heart attack while appearing at a ukulele festival in Massachusetts in 1996. Released from the hospital after three weeks, he was warned to give up his touring and performing. He chose to pursue his art. He suffered a fatal heart attack in Minneapolis on November 30, 1996. He had left the stage after performing his signature song, "Tip-Toe Through the Tulips;" he died an hour later.

As I said before, when anyone asks me, who is the most famous guest we ever had, I am pleased and proud to say it was Tiny Tim!

Kenny Loggins

Kenny Loggins and his new wife were in Denver to promote an upcoming album release. They stayed with us two, maybe three days sort of hiding out from fans. His wife was into fitness, natural food, and such. She would come into our kitchen each morning, get out our food processor and mix up a big batch of dark green stuff for her and Kenny to have for breakfast. She would have none of our breakfasts, they were not healthy enough she said. She would take her so-called breakfast up to their room to eat. She would then get on her Spandex

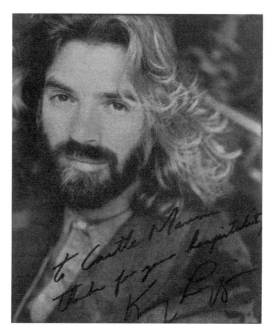
One of our most famous guests; singer,
Kenny Loggins.

outfit, and be off running. As soon as she left, Kenny would stick his head in the kitchen and ask if I would scramble up a big serving of eggs and cheese with onions, toast and muffins. and lots of coffee.

While he said he didn't want any publicity, he offered to sign autographs for our guests. I remember one guest went out and bought a dozen of his albums to give as Christmas gifts and had Kenny sign a personalized message on each of them. Kenny was a very polite and gracious guest. Everyone enjoyed meeting him, not so much his wife. I don't think their marriage lasted very long.

Eddie Vetter

Eddie Vetter stayed with us that same summer. He was in town for a fancy private fund raising event. I believe he was with us just one day. He was very clear that he did not want any publicity or fans bothering him.

We had an innkeeper who apparently was a big Eddie Vetter fan. He walked through the Parlor where Eddie was waiting for his limo to pick him up. Our innkeeper raced into the kitchen and whispered to me, "Do you know who is sitting in our parlor? It's Eddie Vetter." He was actually trembling and could hardly speak. I closed the kitchen door and said, "Yes, it is him. You will not bother him or ask for his autograph, and if you do, I will fire you on the spot, and do I make myself clear?" I don't think my innkeeper ever forgave me. Eddie Vetter was pretty much all business, preferring to keep to himself.

Vicky Hamilton & Salty Dog

Vicky Hamilton worked for a Hollywood record company, traveling and promoting up-and-coming rock bands. She wore yellow cowboy boots, long tattered stockings and had wild crazy hair and make-up. She stayed with us while the band she was promoting stayed at a hotel over on Colfax. This would have been around 1991. One particular group named SALTY DOG has special memories for me. One day she asked if she could bring one of the band members over for Afternoon

Salty Dog, managed by Vicky Hamilton, Hollywood talent scout.

Tea. She introduced him as Booger. As I remember him, he was quite tall with long wild hair, tattoos and bare-chested wearing a ratty vest of sorts. Oh, and he had an electronic tracking monitor locked on his ankle. As fate would have it, that same afternoon, Betsy Webb, one of our regular guests, was also staying with us. She was an entomologist at the Denver Museum of Natural History.

As we were all sitting around the Parlor having Tea and Scones, Booger struck up a conversation with Betsy about birds. He put his hands to his mouth, asking her if she could identify this bird from its call, which he then twittered. Betsy sat bolt upright looking very surprised, and quickly named the bird. She said to him, "Do you know this bird?" For the next 10 or 15 minutes they twittered and quizzed each other while the rest of us sat in stunned silence. It turned out Booger had been an Eagle Scout and earned a merit badge in birdcalls.

Another time, Vicky was in town with different band, but I don't remember its name. One of the rockers asked her to take him to the antique store area down on South Broadway. Later he told this story: As they were walking down the street he heard a little voice saying to him, "Come into this store." Once inside, the voice spoke to him again saying, "Look down on the table in front of you." He looked down and saw a small silver caviar service dish with a hinged cover. Then as its cover opened and closed as if talking, he was told "Take me to the Castle Marne." Well, he bought it and gave it to us as a gift. We subsequently bought two others and have used them on our breakfast table every morning since as butter chip dishes. Vicky and her friends were special, though a bit odd.

Lassie Ahern

I have a couple of old photographs of a silent movie star named Lassie Ahern, who stayed with us during the summer of 1990. She was in Denver visiting family. She was a very dear person and I guess the first and only real movie star who ever stayed with us. She was 70 years old and very bubbly.

In 2016, a newspaper article reported that she was the oldest remaining Our Gang silent movie star personality. She was born in 1920 in Los Angeles and got her start in movies in 1923. Actor Will Rogers recommended to her father that she and her older sister Peggy get into show business. They were early members of the Hal Roach Our Gang Comedy short subjects in the 1920s. She and Peggy were regulars on the burlesque circuit as a singing and dancing sister act. Her most famous film appearance was in Uncle Tom's Cabin, as a young boy. The Lassie Lou Classics clothing line was made by Jean Carol Frocks and was available at most major department stores during the early 1930s. This very special lady stayed with us often that summer. She gave us an original 1930s autographed publicity photo of she and her sister, which reads, "Love to my second family, the adorable Peiker's. Lassie Ahern, July 7, 1990."

Other Interesting Guests

Over the years we have had many other very interesting people stay with us.

Emory Kristof was the chief photographer for Titanica, the 1992 IMAX documentary film about the wreck of the RMS Titanic. He stayed with us when the film opened at the Denver Natural History Museum IMAX Theater. He was a truly fascinating man who left us some wonderful photographs.

Anthony Braxton, an American composer and instrumentalist also stayed at the Castle while he was in Denver in 1991, promoting the first album of his group, The Freewheelers, a rock and roll roots quintet.

Most Unforgettable Guest

While we have had our share of celebrity guests, such as Tiny Tim, Eddie Vetter, Kenny Loggins, and Lassie Ahern; we are often asked who was our most unforgettable guest? After a bit of thought just one really stands out, and I don't even remember his name.

About 15 or 16 years ago, a young man stayed with us while attending the Great American Beer Festival. He announced that he intended to try all of the 1200 beers being judged. After a big night at the show, somehow he made it back to the Castle Marne about 2:30 in the morning. Much the worse for wear, he was still able to get in and up to his third floor room.

My wife and I were living in the Carriage House, just behind the Inn when, at 3:00 a.m. the phone beside our bed rang. It was the guests who were staying in the room on the second floor just below our reveler's room.

A panicky voice shouted, "You'd better get over here, there's a flood." I jumped into my pants and ran barefooted into the Marne. Entering the front door I could see water running out of the ceiling down the wall in the Foyer. I ran upstairs and looked in their room. Sure enough water was cascading through the ceiling of their bathroom. I ran up the stairs to the third floor. Luckily his door was not bolted or chained. Opening the door, I was met with a cloud of steam and the sound of the shower running. I found him naked and passed out in the shower, sitting on the drain.

I turned off the water and rolled him off the drain. I used all the towels and robes to soak up the water. I ran down the stairs to get buckets, fans, and a mop. I moved the guests into a room across the hall. By 5:00 a.m., things were drying out. Luckily there wasn't any permanent damage.

Thankfully none of the other guests were disturbed. Too late to go back to bed, I started preparing breakfast for our guests. As fate would have it, at breakfast that morning, the second floor guests sat across from the reveler. In a friendly voice, they asked, "Wow, how about that flood here last night?" To which he replied, "What flood?"

Bees

One hot June afternoon nine years ago, guests who were staying in the Tower Room up on the third floor, told me there was some clear sticky stuff running down a window casement in their room. They said it looked and smelled like honey.

I went upstairs to look and indeed, it was honey. I got a stepladder, climbed up and carefully cut a hole in the plaster wall above the window. Then with a flashlight, I peered inside to see a honeycomb, with bees busily at work. I quickly closed the hole so that no bees could get into the house. I called a beekeeper to come out and remove the bees. He came out the next day, but was unable to find the queen and move the hive. The only thing he could do was spray the hive with insecticide to kill all the bees. He couldn't give us a reason why the hive was leaking raw honey. We got his bill for services rendered and he left, leaving Louie and me to remove the honey-filled combs and dead bees. Repairing and repainting the wall would come later.

We hauled extension ladders up to the third floor and cut out a large section of plaster wall to expose the hive, which to our dismay was old and quite large. It was buried within the studs and structural components of the original Ballroom construction of 1889. We stripped to the waist and with bare hands began removing the hive, often reaching into the hive up to our armpits. We filled up 5 gallon buckets and emptied them in the alley dumpster. It took us the better part of a day. We lost count, but we must have removed well over 25 gallons of honey-filled combs, which couldn't be saved because of the poison spray.

Lastly, we borrowed a forty-foot extension ladder, climbed up the front of the house and plugged the entrance to the hive, so the bees couldn't get back in. We were told they would try very hard to get back in and rebuild the hive.

We did save a small portion of the combs as souvenirs of that very unpleasant experience.

CHAPTER EIGHTEEN
The Setting
Stage ✤ Cameras ✤ Acclaim

John Hand - *Colorado Free University*

Long active in Capitol Hill neighborhood affairs, John Hand founded Colorado Free University (CFU) in 1987, after Denver Free University went bankrupt. With his family, he bought the historic Park View Hotel, which was built in 1914 at the corner of Colfax and York. In the mid-1980s, he operated an antique store on the corner while renting office space and managing his school out of the building.

CFU was a typical free university, offering a wide variety of subject matter, from cooking classes to gardening, local history and most anything else. He invited people sign up to teach class's on about any subject you could imagine, and the prices were very reasonable.

We had been in business less than a year when John Hand came to our door. He introduced himself as founder and operator of Colorado Free University, and would I be interested in teaching a class on owning and operating a bed and breakfast. He would take care of all the details, from promoting classes, taking reservations, and collecting the money. All I had to do was conduct two-hour classes at our Castle Marne on a Saturday five or six times a year. He would even furnish folding chairs if needed.

I was quite taken aback and told him I had been in business less than a year and was still trying to figure out how to run my own B&B, let alone teach somebody else how to do it. He was insistent that I could do it if I just tried. To make a long story short, it was the beginning of a delightful and mutually productive relationship with John and CFU.

We didn't make a lot of money, but we began to realize that we learned and understood more about the hospitality industry and our place in it. There were marketing opportunities, media exposure while building a sense of industry credibility for us. The old adage was true… we would learn more from our students than they learned from us. The Castle seemed to smile when we shared our story with aspiring innkeepers.

In the beginning, we had to limit class size to twenty-five. Over the years as the economy, communications and our industry changed, we found fewer people were signing up for classes. When class sizes consistently dropped below ten, we felt it was time to get out of the how-to business. Our last classes were offered in 1993.

Looking back, John and his CFU were significant contributors to our early development, evolution and the position in the hospitality business that we enjoy today. Thank you, John.

Father Dowling Mysteries

A month or so after we closed on the property in 1988 and were proud owners of "the big old vacant stone building with the round window," there was a knock on our door. A couple of gentlemen wanted to talk to me about a television series filming location. A local production company had signed up to work on a new TV series to be made in Denver called, "Father Dowling Mysteries." They wanted to film portions of it in our house. They would rebuild the first floor as the residence of a fictional Chicago Catholic priest turned part-time detective, who along with a young nun, would solve all sorts of mysteries. They would pay for everything, all the rebuilding and decorating and rent. It all sounded wonderful, except they wanted me to sign a one-year lease with a second year option. The star of the series would be Tom Bosley, as Father Frank Dowling, with Tracy Nelson as Sister Stephanie, the nun, and Mary Wickes as the housekeeper, Marie. This all sounded wonderful, but, we were going to open our dream bed and breakfast as soon as it was restored and renovated, which I believed would not take very long. So the timing of their wonderful proposal just wouldn't work for us.

I suggested they talk to the Unity Temple, just across the street at 1555 Race. The church was in an old mansion originally built for Delos Chappell, a prominent Denver attorney. Unity Temple had been there since the early 1930s, but was suffering from a serious decline in membership and facing a financial crisis. They had just brought in a new minister to set about closing it down. Father Dowling Mysteries would turn out very well for them. They were able to work out an arrangement whereby the congregation would move out and rent a storefront on Colfax for their church while the movie was filmed in their building. They made enough money over the next year to get back on their feet and today the church is a solid member of our neighborhood community.

Interestingly enough, they did much of the filming at night. They said they were able to control the lighting, etc. When filming, they would close off Race Street at 16th, as well as at Colfax, bring in dressing room trailers, equipment trucks and electrical generating trucks, and park them in the street. Then when it got dark they would set-up huge floodlights and filming would go on most all night. We agreed to let them use our first floor as their break room, where the actors and crew could hang out for coffee and donuts. I charged them $50 a day. It was our first income! A food truck parked out in front and was always ready to serve snacks and fresh meals. We set up tables and chairs inside and got electricity and water turned on for them.

We got to know most of the cast and crew as they hung out at our place. There were between 60 to 70 people involved in the production. They generally filmed for three days, sometimes four. Filming would take place all around town, wherever the script called for. But most of the scenes were shot on our block. It was fascinating to watch a Hollywood production being shot right in our front yard.

About 12 years later, a Denver policeman came by and asked if I remembered the weird noises and strange lights that happened late at night up on our third floor during the Father Dowling filming. I said yes, there was a lot of talk about ghosts and it became quite a topic of conversation. He smiled and said he was the ghost. He had been hired as an off-duty policeman to patrol the block while they were here. He went on to say, now and then, late at night, he would get bored and sneak upstairs and make strange noises, flashing his light around and dropping pebbles down the stairs. The show filmed the first year here, then moved to Hollywood to do the last two years of production.

If Walls Could Talk

I believe it was early summer of 1998, when Tom Giesen came to our door. He was a TV producer and his company was going to produce a new series named "If Walls Could Talk." They needed a location to produce the introduction and conclusion of the programs. It seems Tom lived east of us in Park Hill and most every day rode his bicycle down 16th Avenue to his downtown office. Today he decided to check us out. After looking around the first floor, he said we were perfect for the filming. So began another remarkable TV experience for our Castle Marne.

The show website read: "If Walls Could Talk discovers the mysteries lurking beneath homes' surfaces and puts a price on history. The award-winning series profiles homeowners from across the country who renovate their historic homes and uncover unusual stories and valuable objects along the way. From century-old diaries to rare coins to even an unopened bank vault, these unexpected discoveries are a lesson in history for thrilled homeowners. Selected homeowners also get the shock of a lifetime when our expert appraiser drops in to tell them that what they found is worth a fortune."

The film crew would come in and take-over the Foyer and Parlor with cameras, lights, cable, and such. On cue, the host would sweep out of the Foyer into the Parlor saying, "Welcome to another program of If Walls Could Talk." He would go on to say that today we are going to the former home of President Zachary Taylor and show you the wonderful secrets they discovered. Then he would sweep out again saying he hoped everyone enjoyed the show and would join them next week when they visit a home containing an ink sketch of Walt Disney.

After two seasons of filming, I began to ask when we might be featured. Finally, I wore them down and they agreed to do an episode about our Castle Marne. Imagine that big old stone building with the round window on National TV. For the filming, I walked around describing the pedestal in the parlor, the window, the 1890s photographs, Mr. Lang, and general history of the neighborhood and house.

Starkey Institute

About the time we opened for business, a woman named Mary Starkey opened her business, the Starkey International Institute of Household Management. It was in a wonderful old mansion built in 1897, known as the House of a Thousand Candles, at 1410 High Street, just down the street from us. It was the first and only recognized school of its kind in the country, and still is I believe. We got to know her and became close friends, being in the same sort of business. We joked that it was Butler Boot Camp. Mary would have a Formal Dinner at the end of each term where students were graded on setting, seating, serving, clearing and all other specific procedures. Diane and I were privileged to attend many of these dinners.

In late 1992, she hired a gentleman named Lee Whiteway as headmaster of the school. He had served as chef and butler to a bevy of luminaries, including former presidents Nixon, Carter and Ford, Mayor Koch, Estee Lauder, Jacqueline Onassis, Princess Lee Radziwill, Andy Warhol, Barbara Walters, and Bob and Delores Hope. A flamboyant gentleman, he would bring a smile to your face as he would sashay down the street in his full length coyote fur coat flowing in the breeze. Mary moved her school to 1350 Logan Street around the turn of the century.

But now the rest of the story....

Country Inns Magazine - *Christmas in July*

We were contacted by the *Country Inns* magazine to be a part of their 1993 Christmas issue. The editor was a friend of Lee Whiteway and the article would be about Castle Marne and The Starkey Institute of School of Household Management. We all got together over the next few months to get a plan together. As it finally worked out, we would host a grand costumed Christmas Tea party here in our parlor served by Mary's students. Lee was also featured instructing his students in the proper way to make a bed. The magazine's deadline for the Christmas issue was the end of July, which meant decorating the house for Christmas in the middle of summer. It was our responsibility to hire a photographer and furnish photographs of everything to the magazine. We ended up hiring a photographer who was a friend of a friend who could start immediately. Our neighbors were a bit concerned when I was stringing lights and hanging wreaths in July. The Holiday Tea party was something to behold. Everyone was dressed in period costumes, the house fully decorated and the table set for a king. The Starkey student wait-staff were dressed to the nines and the photographer clicked away. Everything had to be in the hands of the magazine editor that Monday morning. The party was held Friday night and raw film was boxed and sent express to New York late Friday night. Saturday morning we started taking the decorations down and getting back to normal. At 6:00 am Monday morning the phone rang. It was the editor calling from New York. The photographer had used a filter and something had gone wrong; the pictures could not be used. We didn't know what happened and didn't have time to worry about it. The magazine had to have new pictures in their hands the next Monday morning. No excuses or no article. The photographer was fired. I hired another photographer, scheduled Mary's students, decorated the house again and re-shot the whole thing over by Friday. The new photographer did a truly amazing job. She developed the film Friday night to be certain all was perfect and sent the film to New York. The editor called Monday at 6:00 a.m. and raved about the pictures. He told me the original four-page spread was increased to six pages. The year 1993 is remembered as the year we decorated for Christmas three times.

Lingerie Catalog

About a year, maybe two, after opening, we were approached by a family, who had a women's lingerie shop in Grand Junction, Colorado. A couple of them had worked for Victoria's Secret. They wanted to get into the mail-order catalog business. This was before the Internet. They had searched around for a classy, Victorian mansion to film their first catalog. I don't know how they found us, but they did and we needed exposure, no pun intended.

I don't remember how much we charged them, if at all. It turned out they were a good Mormon family including three sisters and a brother who all posed, costumed, and handled make-up and staging. We were told their photographer was a church friend; it all went off without a hitch. They were all young, attractive, very dedicated, polite and talented artists. It didn't come off as lurid or sexy, but was quite professional. It took three days to do the shoot. We were not very busy, so the shooting didn't cause us many problems and it really was something to watch. A few pictures from their finished catalog will show you what I mean. I don't remember if we ever heard from them again.

Publications: Magazines:

1990   *Elegant Lingerie*
1990   *Insider - Country Inns, B&B's, and Historic Travel*
1991   *Old-House Journal*
1993   *Lark Ballastic (Samsonite) Luggage Catalog*
1993   *Country Inns Bed & Breakfast*
1993   *Abenteuer & Reisen (a German Travel magazine)*
1994   *5280 Magazine*
1994   *America West-Airlines Magazine*
1994   *Colorado Homes & Lifestyles*
1994   *Country Inns Bed & Breakfast*
1994   *Bon Appetit*
1994   *Travel Agent*
1994   *Mature Choices*
1995   *Victorian Life Styles*
1995   *Bride's Magazine*
1995   *5280*
1996   *5280*
1997   *Canadian Doctor's Review*
1997   *Empire Magazine of the West - The Denver Post*
1997   *Sunset - The Magazine of Western Living*
1999   *Frontier Airline Magazine*
1999   *The Motorist - AAA*
1999   *The Denver Boulder Catalogue*
2000   *The Motorist - AAA*
2017   *Knitting Traditions*

Publications: News

1989   *Historic Denver News*
1989   *LIFE on Capitol Hill*
1989   *The Denver Post*
1990   *The Daily Journal*
1990   *University of Denver News*
1991   *Los Angeles Times*

1991 *The New York Times - Travel*

1992 *The Denver Business Journal*

1992 *The Columbus Dispatch - Travel*

1993 *Rocky Mountain News - Spotlight*

1993 *Rocky Mountain News - Sunday*

1992 *The Denver Business Journal*

1992 *LIFE on Capitol Hill*

1993 *Colorado Woman News*

1995 *The Denver Post*

1995 *The Denver Business Journal*

1995 *USA Today*

1995 *Rocky Mountain News - Spotlight*

1996 *USA Today- Life*

1997 *The New York Times*

1999 *The Denver Post*

2000 *The Denver Business Journal*

2002 *Rocky Mountain News*

2002 *Colorado Adventure*

2008 *Denver & the West*

2011 *Your Hub*

2013 *Neighborhood Life*

2015 *The New York Times, "One Day in Denver-Best B&B"*

2017 *The Denver Post, "Most Romantic Valentine's Dinner in Denver"*

CHAPTER NINETEEN

The Neighborhood
Community Influx ✤ Community Action
Community Power

Gangs

When we bought the property in 1988, we were aware of the neighborhood's history of hippies and counter-culture, but gave little thought to organized gang activity. A year or so after we opened, we began to notice more and more gang activity in the neighborhood. We often discussed it at Colfax on the Hill (COTH) Merchants Association meetings and with the police department. It appeared to be centered at a local nightclub called Obsession 21, on the corner of Colfax and Gaylord, just two blocks away. Problems continued to escalate and worsen. Finally in the spring of 1991, with help from Capitol Hill United Neighborhoods (CHUN), a group of neighbors gathered together and started meeting regularly. In June, a meeting was held with the attorney of the nightclub and a neighborhood agreement was signed concerning their practices and their customers' activities. While it had little legal force, we all hoped for the best. But as summer passed, the crime and gang activity got worse and worse.

Diane and I were living in the manager's quarters, now our 10th rental room, named the Holland Suite, which looked out over the parking lot on the alley. One night about 2:00 a.m., I heard some noises in back. I got out of bed and looked out the window to see two kids hot wiring a car in our parking lot. I called the police and waited. The police arrived just about the same time the kids got the car running and started racing down the alley. They crashed the car into a telephone pole, jumped out, and escaped. The car belonged to one of our guests. Apparently, to be initiated into the gang you had to steal a car to prove yourself.

That same summer, a guest of ours finished breakfast with his wife and excused himself from the table. He had a couple of customers to call on and would be back later to pick her up. A few minutes later he came back and asked his wife where they had parked their car last night. It wasn't in our parking lot. I called the police and reported their car stolen. The police got back a couple of hours later, they found the car abandoned about 20 miles north of Denver, out of gas and undamaged.

Finally the Denver Department of Excise and Licenses stepped up, and mailed this letter to the neighborhood:

"Dear Neighbor of Obsession 21,

Thank you for your letters, information, and support of the matter of Obsession 21. As you probably know the Department of Excise and Licenses and Bamboo Gardens, Inc. doing business as Obsession 21, have reached an agreement. The cabaret license for Obsession 21 will be surrendered on January 20, 1992. I hope this will solve most of the problems you have been experiencing.

Sincerely,

Mary Sylvester,

Director of Excise and Licenses

November 19, 1991."

Sad to say, the gang just moved three blocks west.

The Squire Lounge at Williams and Colfax, three blocks away, had been a hangout for undesirables for several years. I finally wrote the mayor.

"Dear Mayor Webb,

This letter describes my concerns pertaining to the Squire Lounge and to the needs and desires of the neighborhood. I appreciate your interest and concern and strongly urge that their liquor license not be renewed. I await your reply.

Sincerely, Jim Peiker

January 21, 1992."

The mayor's response is as follows:

"Dear Mr. Peiker,

Thank you for your letter dated January 21, 1992, about the Squire Lounge. The Director of Excise and Licenses informs me that she has accepted the decision of the renewing officer, pending ten days for comments. The hearing officer recommended that the license not be renewed.

Thank you for writing to me with your concerns. I hope that our actions will be helpful to you. As you know my administration remains committed to creating an environment in which small businesses like yours will flourish.

Yours truly,

Wellington Webb, Mayor

February 6, 1992."

They say hope springs eternal, but in this case, the gangs just moved again to the IHOP at Race and Colfax, the other end of our block. Through the spring and summer things went from bad to worse. They didn't have a liquor license, so we couldn't use the same tactics. Every Thursday, Friday, and Saturday night, around 2:30 am, after the bars and clubs closed, the gangs would come from around town and meet in the IHOP parking lot to hang out, sell drugs, and generally raise hell. We and the B&B across the street were the only full-time residents on the 1500 block of Race Street. The rest of the buildings were businesses that weren't here for the night time fireworks. Consequently, they and other business and property owners were not overly concerned.

The mayor and the police had begun to have serious gang problems in other parts of town and weren't able to focus on our problems. Now and then fights would break out and there was occasional gunfire. The manager of the IHOP refused to do anything, as he said the gangs were a large part of his business. The city said they would do what they could. IHOP Corporate was little help because they supported their franchisee. We complained bitterly to friends who were on City Council. They got behind what would be Denver's first meaningful Nuisance Abatement Ordinance and got it passed. Its first application was against the IHOP.

As fate would have it, the city had authorized a 6th Police District, which included us. Finally we hoped to get meaningful police response. District 6 set out to use the new ordinance to force the IHOP to act against the gangs. It seemed to take forever, but they finally ruled that IHOP would have to increase lighting of the parking lot and pay for street barriers, which were set up every Thursday, Friday, and Saturday nights, on 16th Avenue and on Colfax, to discourage the gangs. They also required additional off-duty officers on those nights.

Our neighborhood group got together to build a case. Around 2:00 o'clock in the morning, Diane and I would sit on our front porch and count the number of cars full of troublemakers on their way to the IHOP and report on activities to the police. A neighbor across the alley from the parking lot began to film the activity each night. The troublemakers would simply move the barriers and drive down to the IHOP. If the lot filled up, they would leave their cars in the middle of the street. The District 6 officers told us we would have to convince the gangs to find another location to meet and party. Finally, each night when the gang cars began coming down the street, police cars would park bumper to front bumper along our street and at alleys and streets accessing the 1500 block of Race to turn away the cars and make them go somewhere else. It took weeks of this until the gangs got the message and went elsewhere, finally leaving us alone.

Capitol Hill United Neighbors (CHUN) and the Colfax Business Improvement District (CBID), worked closely with the Guardian Angels and District 6 Police. Working together, we have been able to substantially control organized gang activity in our neighborhood since then.

The Parking Lot that Glowed

Around World War I, uranium was mined in the mountains west of Denver. It was believed that exposure to radon gas from radium would cure arthritis, crippled legs, and all sorts of illnesses. I vividly remember in the late 1940s, riding with my family through Idaho Springs and seeing old gold mines with large signs proclaiming the healing powers of radium and inviting everyone with all manner of aches and pains to COME IN AND BE CURED. Large piles of canes, crutches and old wheelchairs stacked around the mine entrances proclaiming it was true.

The story of radium is told right here on Race Street. In 1891, at 1524 Race Street, a mansion designed by William Lang was built for a lawyer named Harry Lindsley. He lived there until World War I, when he sold it to the Rocky Mountain Radium Institute for their headquarters. Denver became known as the radium capitol of the world. In addition to office space for the institute, radium for commercial, cosmetics, and health purposes was refined there. Some said that numbers and decoration on watch faces were painted with radium in this facility as well. The slag, or dross, which was left after the chemical was refined, was dumped in the backyard, buried and forgotten.

Radium mining and processing declined during the 1920s and was generally forgotten by the 1930s. The mansion continued to be used as general office space into the 1970s, when it was torn down to provide a parking lot for the soon to be built IHOP on the corner of Colfax and Race. In the fall of 1992, the entire corner, parking lot and building, was declared a Superfund Site. Surprisingly the EPA said it was polluted with highly radioactive material and a danger to the neighborhood and the world. Spring arrived and so did the abatement workers. Dressed in full hazmat suits, they installed a 10-foot chain link fence around the property with flood lights everywhere. Large signs warned the world to stay clear or you would be exposed to dangerous radioactive material. There were signs warning that vicious attack dogs were guarding the property 24-hours a day. They began removing the entire parking lot, down to what looked to be 12-feet deep.

It was underneath the IHOP building as well. They put large timbers under the corners of the restaurant to support the building as they dug all the dirt out from under it. They worked 24-hours a day, seven days a week, all of that summer. Watching from a safe distance, it was quite a sight to behold. The contaminated dirt was loaded into special semi-trucks with a clam-shell-like cover to tightly seal against radioactive leakage. Locked shut, it was driven nonstop to the Dugway Proving Grounds in the Utah salt flats for storage and supervision. The restaurant was closed during the excavation. The IHOP was well compensated for the loss of revenue. The excavation site was filled in with safe dirt and paved over. So much for the parking lot that glowed...

The Guru Maharaji Ji

The home next door to us on the south side has a unique history. In 1887, Wilbur Raymond purchased all the lots on the east side of Race Street to Colfax. In 1890 he built his home on the corner of Race and 16th Ave. He sold the remaining lots to George Titcomb, who hired William Lang to design houses for each of the properties. The house stood vacant for several years due to the 1893 Depression. It was income property as an apartment building in the ensuing years.

In the late 1960s, it became a yoga commune and eventually world headquarters for the Divine Light Mission Church. The church was built around a 14 year-old East Indian boy known as Satgurudev Shri, as well as Prem Pal Singh Rawat, or Guru Maharaj Ji. He, along with his mother and older brother, lived in the mansion. Hippies, Hari-Krishna, Moonies, and other such folks perpetuated the image of a Haight-Ashbury here in Denver. In 1972 the church moved to a more prestigious address in Denver's Hilltop neighborhood. A few years later the church relocated to Malibu, California. The church is alive and well with several million adherents worldwide.

Pete's Wicked Ale

During the 1992 Great American Beer Festival here in Denver, we had folks from Pete's Wicked Ale staying with us. Their brewery was just a few years old and hadn't won many awards. They were off early to the show every morning, working hard to be the rising star in the craft beer community. They were looking for the gold. I will never forget that on the last day of the show, they had been awarded the Gold Medal first prize for their signature American Brown Ale. They came back to the Castle that afternoon flying high! They were soon out on the front lawn tossing around a football and shouting loudly about winning the Gold. I seem to remember they were consuming a bit of their Gold Medal winner as well. A neighbor down the block later told us, you could smell the testosterone all the way to Colfax. It was great fun to be a part of such a well-deserved victory celebration.

The Easter Bunny

Oh all right, just one more. I recently stumbled on this memory, complete with newspaper photo.

It appeared in the *Rocky Mountain News* before Easter, 1992. Tillie Fong, was the staff writer:

"Who knows what creature strikes the planters of Race Street late at night? The Easter Bunny knows. A colorful trail of plastic eggs, weather vanes and inflatable bunnies and ducks has been left, on recent nights, in front of homes, inns and offices in the 1500 block of Race Street. Residents are both puzzled and delighted. "I think it's kind of neat," said Ralph Heronema, 33, of 1515 Race St. He became the latest target, of the mysterious decorator Tuesday. Heronema said he got up at 6 am Tuesday and saw two inflatable bunnies, a male in blue overalls with a carrot and a female in a pink polka dot dress, lashed to the pillars of his front porch. 'Nobody has a clue on who's doing this,' Heronema says. 'We have a mad Easter Bunny on the loose,' he said. The mysterious being first made its presence known two weeks ago to Clyde Stephens, 34, co-owner of the Victoria Oaks Inn at 1575 Race St, who got hit with a pink flamingo in one of his planters.

'I think it's a new kind of gang and this is how they do a neighborhood', he said jokingly. On Sunday, two other places on the historic block were hit with plastic Easter eggs and other objects. Tuesday, the mystery decorator also hit an office building, along with Heronema's historic Milheim House. So far, everyone is enjoying the mystery.

'It just points out that this neighborhood has a heart and a sense of humor,' said Jim Peiker, 57, owner of Castle Marne, 1572 Race St. 'It's a good place to live.'"

The Vagnino Family

Josephine Vagnino purchased 1560 Race Street from the Divine Light Mission in 1976 for $65,000. She and her two sons, John Jr. and Richard, lived there for many years. John Sr. started what is now known as American Beauty Macaroni Co. in the family's kitchen in North Denver around 1900. A factory was built in North Denver and business flourished. In 1912, the then Denver Macaroni Company merged with the Kansas City Macaroni Company to become American Beauty. John Sr. died in 1952. His wife Josephine died fifty years later, John Jr. died ten years ago. Younger brother Richard continued to live alone on the third floor of the house until a serious fire occurred on December 6, 2014. As of this writing, a luxury three-unit condominium is planned for the burned out shell.

Capitol Hill United Neighborhoods

It was 1969, when a group of concerned citizens rallied to prevent the proposed conversion of East 11th and 12th avenues into one-way streets. The victory of the citizens over city planners marked the beginning of what is now known as Capitol Hill United Neighborhoods Inc. (CHUN), one of Denver's oldest and largest Registered Neighborhood Organizations (RNO). An outgrowth of those first meetings was a neighborhood celebration.

Held in the playground of Morey Junior High School in May of 1972, the first People's Fair was a success and plans were made to stage the fair the following year. By 1976, the fair had out grown the playground and was moved to the Esplanade in front of East High School. Its popularity continued to grow and by 1986, an estimated 200,000 people attended the Fair. It was time to move again, this time to Denver's Civic Center Park, where it continues hold forth yearly on the first weekend of May.

CHUN provides a democratic forum for discussing many neighborhood issues, including liquor licensing, historic preservation, crime prevention, environmental concerns, neighborhood beautification, street maintenance, education, and traffic control. The Tree Committee has beautified Capitol Hill by giving away thousands of free trees over the years. The CHUN mission is, "Preserving the Past, Improving the Present and Planning for the Future of Greater Capitol Hill." Our Historic Preservation Committee has helped establish over 20 historic preservation districts and assisted in designation of over a dozen individual properties. The CHUN Historic Preservation Committee continues to meet each month in the Dining Room of the Castle Marne. It is deeply involved in preserving our neighborhoods' architectural and historic character and ambience.

After 21 years, I retired from the CHUN Board of Directors, but continued to serve on the preservation committee. At the 2010 annual meeting, I was awarded the Tom Knorr Good Neighbor Award. At the same meeting, the annual Historic Preservation Award was named the James R. Peiker Award For Historic Preservation. This was truly an unexpected and appreciated honor.

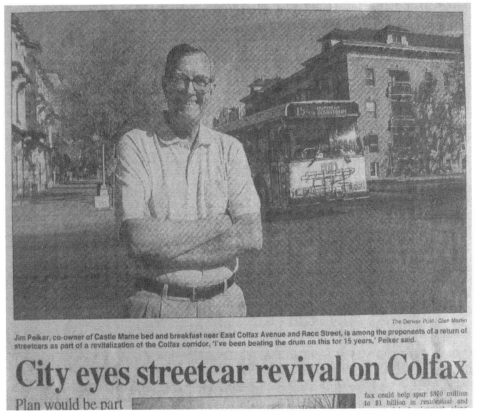

The Denver Post / Glen Martin

Jim Peiker, co-owner of Castle Marne bed and breakfast near East Colfax Avenue and Race Street, is among the proponents of a return of streetcars as part of a revitalization of the Colfax corridor. 'I've been beating the drum on this for 15 years,' Peiker said.

City eyes streetcar revival on Colfax

Plan would be part ... fax could help spur $400 million to $1 billion in residential and

Jim promoting the return of the Colfax street car, *The Denver Post.*

Colfax on the Hill and CBID

Colfax on the Hill, (COTH) Inc. is a volunteer business association of property and business owners, managers, and associate members. They work to promote retail business and office space occupancy, attract new businesses and services, and engage in the overall economic development and revitalization of the East Colfax corridor, between Broadway and Colorado Boulevard, from 14th Avenue to 16th Avenue.

The mission is to clean up the district's streets, alleys and storefronts, reduce crime, and increase the desirability of the district as a place to locate a business or office and to promote the desirability of the district for shopping, dining, and entertainment. It has been a matter of enlightened self-interest and commitment to the community. The credo is, "You can make a difference! Only through a unified, concerted and constant effort can we continue the effort and mission of transforming Colfax into a safe and thriving Main Street."

We joined COTH at about the same time we joined CHUN, adding a business-oriented component to our neighborhood involvement. Marty Amble was named by the City to be its first Executive Director. He served for three years and then remained involved in the community as an active member.

Margo Hartman, owner of the Holiday Chalet B&B, served as first president of COTH. Under her leadership, with the cooperation of the Regional Transportation Department and Cherry Creek Shopping Center, she established The Cultural Connection Trolley. It was a rubber-tired trolley, which ran a regularly scheduled route from downtown, east along Colfax and south on York Street to the Cherry Creek Shopping Center. It was intended to highlight businesses along Colfax, showing the neighborhood as a viable retail district. It was a good try, but was discontinued two years later.

COTH continues to be an important stabilizing factor along the Colfax corridor. In the beginning, the Colfax Business Improvement District, which was supported by a business property tax, was an arm of COTH. In later years, it broke away and serves as an independent body, the Colfax Business Improvement District (CBID). Melissa served as Chairman for three years and a board member for eleven years.

Uptown on the Hill

In 1983, Ed Natan took the lead in helping form Uptown on the Hill neighborhood association (UOTH). He is responsible for the name, he said, "We have a downtown, this is Denver's Uptown."

British Double Decker Bus tours were offered, describing the history and architectural sights of Uptown. Its boundaries were Broadway to York, Colfax to 20th. North Capitol Hill tried to establish its ties to downtown. It wanted to emerge as the heart of a new vibrant neighborhood directly associated with the downtown business community, with its charms, history, landmark buildings, and Victorian architecture.

LIFE on Capitol Hill, 1989

"Denver's Uptown On The Hill is the place to go out, the place to visit and the place to stay. It's fun; it's varied and it's happening, day and night. You can find restaurants, galleries, theatres, shops, services, hotels, key government buildings, parks, a zoo, athletic facilities, hospitals, banks, and places to live, work, lease and buy. It's all within walking distance and next to downtown and the Civic Center." Rocky Mountain News, (September 29, 1996)

"The Peikers are but one example of the rebirth and renovation occurring in Uptown. Peiker said there is both an energy and synergy running through Uptown. The ball is rolling! From single professionals to young families, Uptown has something for everyone. From City Park with its golf course and new playground, to the Zoo and the Museum of Natural History. Peiker said there is a lot of excitement in his neighborhood. New developments and redevelopments will seal the fate of Uptown."

The Uptown Sampler began in 1988, featuring restaurants and businesses mainly along 17th Avenue. It was Denver's first major evening culinary and entertainment event. On one evening in September, folks could sample food and drink served outdoors on the sidewalk, weather permitting.

We all remembered the reputation our neighborhood had gained through the years of feeling unsafe, especially at night. We had to give people an opportunity and a reason to come back and enjoy our neighborhood and feel safe and comfortable. Several British Double Decker Buses traveled the neighborhood dropping off and picking folks up at well-marked and lighted corners. Many people were experiencing the smells, sights, and sounds of our Uptown neighborhood for the first time. We had posters made, welcoming visitors into our businesses. I still have an UPTOWN SAMPLER BUS STOP sign. The Sampler started at 5:00 p.m. and stopped at 9:00 p.m. There was a final loop at 10:00 p.m to pick up any stragglers. Over the years the annual Sampler more than accomplished its goal. It transformed our neighborhood and gave it a new and vibrant reputation. The Sampler has changed some with the neighborhood re-development, but continues, on a September evening, to present the uniqueness of Denver's Uptown neighborhood, continuing to bring a welcome breath of fresh air and vitality.

I guess that some of you are wondering why it took so many civic organizations to handle the various problems. Suffice it to say, the neighborhood; 1st Avenue to 20th Avenue, Broadway to Colorado Boulevard had a lot of problems, from zoning issues to historic preservation to liquor licensing. Colfax was changing. The neighborhood was growing for the first time in many years. Denver was changing and our neighborhood was right in the middle of it.

Being native Denverites, we thought we knew about the problems, Boy, were we ill- informed. It took a little while to begin to realize the problems were many and varied. The neighborhood itself was grappling and coming to solutions and understandings. We began to realize that while there were problems, the people coming together as a community could begin to solve the differences and changes and form a unified and powerful force.

Yes, it was the people, with a spirit unique to our broadly based economic, racial, religious, and cultural differences, who came together as a wonderful and powerful force of change. "It takes a village."

We are here because of the history and architecture, but most of all the people.

We are so very proud of the small contribution our family has made to this wonderful place we call home.

Man of the Year 1993

Each January, *LIFE on Capitol Hill,* the neighborhood monthly newspaper selects its Man and Woman of the Year. For 1993, I was selected as the outstanding man and Lucy Walker as the outstanding woman.

Beneath charcoal sketches of us, done by Walt Young, our neighborhood barber, the following was written by Rory Seeber, editor.

HE'S NOT AFRAID OF THE DIRTY WORK

"Jim Peiker is a soft-spoken, affable and courteous man. He is also driven, frankly outspoken and a supporter of Capitol Hill, who puts his actions where others merely put their words. For these and many other reasons, Jim is *LIFE's* 1993 Man of the Year. Many know him as the owner of Castle Marne, 1572 Race, the four-year old, yet nationally-recognized, Bed and Breakfast.

Community leaders and careful readers of *LIFE* will also know Jim as a tireless worker for the betterment of Capitol Hill. Jim's involvement with the inner-workings of Hill politics and community organizations is a textbook example of how best to get involved, be it as an innkeeper or a force for change.

In the 1970's and 1980's, much of Uptown could be categorized as a demilitarized zone. Sleazy bars, vacant lots and abandoned buildings defined many of the neighborhoods bordering the north edge of East Colfax. Castle Marne in many ways epitomized the sorry state of the neighborhood. Vacant for many years, the once magnificent 1889 William Lang building had become a massive eyesore frequented by vagrants and vandals. Then Jim and his wife Diane, stumbled upon the structure. Unemployed after 20 years on the road selling everything from watches to potting soil to garage door openers, Jim used his congenial sales skills to convince bankers and the Small Business Administration to finance the purchase and refurbishment of the property at a cost of more than $500,000, including most all of the Peiker's life savings. Four years later, the Victorian masterpiece, lovingly attended by Jim with his wife, Diane, daughter, Melissa and her husband Louis, has just been named one of the 12 best inns nationwide by *Country Inns Magazine*. How could Jim envision such a project? His two decades of travel had taught him that it is the personal touch that makes a difference.

A 1953 graduate of South High School and with a 1957 degree from the University of Denver, Jim's travels had taught him that guests enjoy feeling at home more than merely having a bed. His years on the road had also given him a stock of stories and anecdotes to entertain his guests and Jim loves to have a good time. Always ready with a good laugh or an ebullient smile, he can often be found in the Castle's Victorian parlor sharing a joke with his guests. That is, of course, when he isn't attending dozens of neighborhood meetings. Jim has done what any smart businessman should do to succeed. He didn't just move into the neighborhood four years ago, he made it his own. At practically any meeting of Uptown On The Hill, Colfax On The Hill, The Uptown Partnership or Capitol Hill United Neighborhood, just to name the major players, you will find Jim. He is there not only to observe or be seen. He actively participates.

When the Wyman Historic District was ratified after three years of grueling work and frustration. The ratification three months ago, was due in large part to Jim's stewardship and support. Along with many others too numerous to mention, Jim worked tirelessly in support of the effort, hosting meetings, chairing committees and, as always, asking probing questions. For despite his friendly nature and at times bemused appearance, Jim Peiker has never been afraid of speaking his mind to anyone about anything. When residents along 16th Avenue complained to the city about the removal of some traffic lights, Jim was ready to tell anyone about the lethargy and duplicity of the Traffic Department, including the officials themselves. An outspokenness that so readily supports Capitol Hill, is the real reason Jim Peiker is the Man of the Year. His wonderful efforts at restoring Castle Marne notwithstanding, it is the fact that he hasn't been afraid to take on bureaucracy for the betterment of his neighborhood, that makes him someone worthy of our acclaim."

Sketch of Jim as *LIFE on Capitol Hill's* Man of the Year, 1993.

PART FOUR

The Family

CHAPTER TWENTY

Generation 1

Jim and Diane Peiker

Looking back after 28 years of dreams shattered and fulfilled, struggles, disappointments, and successes, we are still a close and loving family unit spanning three generations of Peikers and Feher-Peikers. Now moving forward with a mindful eye on the new opportunities of our travel industry, ever looking to new ventures and challenges, yet always mindful of where we came from. We remember what has made us who we are and what we have become. With confidence, and Tom Teague our Vice President of Finance, and his wife Louise, we are looking forward to a remarkable future lying ahead for us.

"We now move forward in great and gallant company," *Sir Winston Churchill*

Both Diane and I were born and raised in Denver. She grew up near 6th and Humboldt, just 2 blocks from Cheesman Park. She was the oldest of 4 children born to Dorothea O'Leary Carpenter and Lester Griffin Carpenter. Her mother was a housewife, her father a lawyer and real estate developer. Diane attended Dora Moore Elementary School, Morey Junior High, the first year of high school at East, second at Kent, and senior year at South High School, where we met.

I was raised in the 1200 block of South Ogden Street, just 2 blocks from Washington Park. I was the younger of two children born to Helen Sullivan Peiker and Edwin William Peiker. My brother Eddie was two years older. Mother was a housewife and father, the General Manager of the Continental Paper Products Company. I attended McKinley Elementary School, Grant Junior High, and South High School, in the graduating class of 1953.

Diane entered Denver University, where she joined Pi Beta Phi Sorority, graduating in the class of 1957 with an education degree. She was a teacher in elementary grades in Denver Public Schools for four years, then she taught 20 years at St. Mary's Academy.

I went to Colorado University and pledged Sigma Chi Fraternity. The next year I transferred to DU, and graduated with Diane in 1957, with a degree in business administration. Diane and I dated in high school and college and were married on December 15th, 1956, in our senior year. I worked seven years as a salesman for the Continental Paper Products Company, located in Colonel Platt's old paper mill building. I spent the next 25 years selling securities, life insurance, electric garage door openers, garage doors and finally, with a manufacturers rep group, selling all kinds of stuff all over the Rocky Mountain region.

While I had a succession of employment opportunities, Diane had our two children, Melissa, born July 9, 1959, and Riley, born December 31, 1962. After raising them to school age, she went back to teaching at St. Mary's Academy in Englewood. Melissa attended there as a fifth grader, graduating eight years later, in the class of 1978. Riley attended Regis Jesuit High School, graduating in the class of 1980.

Even after we opened our Castle Marne B&B, Diane continued to teach at St. Mary's for three more years, as we needed her salary and insurance benefits. After we would finish preparing and serving breakfast to our guests, she would walk to the bus stop on York Street and catch the bus to St. Mary's, arriving back after school. I was house-keeper, innkeeper, gardener, and general jack-of-all-trades while she was teaching. We are still a great team.

Melissa and her husband, Louie, had no children for 5 years after we opened. Diane and I had the sense that the Castle and our B&B business would substitute for grandchildren. But then in rapid succession, there were three grandchildren and they were all raised in the Castle Marne.

We often have grandparents who come to Denver to visit their grandchildren. Many only see their grandchildren once or twice a year. Diane and I were able to love and hug and kiss our three grandchildren every day. What a special privilege it was for both of us, and how fortunate we were to have the kids as an integral part of our lives. Growing up in our business, they got to meet and experience all kinds of people from all over the world, at an impressionable age.

Jim and Diane

The Red Bug

I really thought I had covered all of the really important stories. But I realize I have left out a meaningful story. It goes back 61 years, it's about Diane and me and our two children and our relationship to the Castle, and it continues today.

I had been driving a 1954 MG bucket seat roadster. There were questions from Dorothea, my new mother-in-law, about where were her grandchildren were going to sit. Besides which, the MG was a mechanical money pit. So, a few months after our wedding in 1956, Diane and I flew to California where we purchased a new, shiny, red VW sedan and drove it home. Over the years we drove the bug everywhere with kids and dogs, carrying groceries and bags of cement, lumber, and whatever else.

Over the next 45 years the paint peeled off, the body rusted, the interior upholstery was sagging and threadbare, and the seats were held together with duct tape. All in all, it was an appalling sight. Mechanically it was still running well, considering it had given some-where between 450-500 thousand miles of reliable service.

I think you know how I feel about dilapidated old relics. A friend of a friend knew a guy who had a used car lot in Englewood who told us he knew some people who could make it look like new again, for a good price. He told me to park the car at his office, push the keys through the mail slot. He would shop it around and get back to me in a couple of weeks. I waited two-three weeks and began to call, but got no response. Then one day, about five weeks later, I got a call from a person who asked if my name was James Peiker. I said, yes and what was this about. The young man then related an amazing story. He worked at an auto upholstery shop about a mile from the auto dealer's office. Every day on his way to work he rode his bike past this rusty old red VW parked on the street. One day he saw a note on the window and he stopped and read, "If this car is not removed at once, it will be towed away to the crusher." A name and number was attached. He called and inquired about the VW and was told he could have it and tow it away, for all they cared, which he did that very afternoon. Some days later as he was stripping out the interior, he found an old dirty rumpled gas receipt in the trash under the front seat with my name on it. He said he could barely read the name, but was able to make it out and he contacted me. Thoughts were going through my head as I drove out to see him. He might not have noticed or bothered with the note on the window, he might not ever have found the receipt, he well could not have called me and he could have kept the car. But he did call. I thanked him profusely and as we talked it was very evident that he was pleased to have found the proper owner of the car. Well, to make a long story shorter, I asked his company to replace the entire interior, headliner, seats, door panels, floors; essentially everything. I also asked if he knew anyone who could do the exterior. Yes he did. Over the next few months both of them virtually made a new Red Bug, inside and out.

Notice anything familiar about this story?

Three things Jim loves the most: Diane, their Red 1957 VW Bug, and Castle Marne.

Jim's Family

My mother's family was Irish and they settled in eastern Indian Territory, now Oklahoma, first in Pawnee, then in the town of Pryor Creek, during the late 1880s. There were six children in her family and she was the youngest. Her mother died in childbirth in 1904, when she was born. Her father died a few years later, but I never knew his cause of death. I am named after him, James Riley Sullivan. Of the six children, mother was the only one whose marriage yielded children. As far as I know, Eddie, my older brother, and I are the only children to carry forth the Sullivan family heritage.

My mother's brother Grover died of wounds suffered in World War I service in France. It was said he was the first soldier from Oklahoma to die in the war. I have been told that as a baby, her brothers and sisters would put mother in a basket under a tree while they picked crops to earn a living.

Mother left Oklahoma when she was around 17 years old moving to Denver. Living at the YWCA, she got a job as a steno at the Continental Label, Litho & Folding Paper Box Company, located at 18th and Blake in Downtown Denver. The building still stands.

There she met my father; they were married on April 26, 1926. They purchased 1221 S. Ogden Street in 1933, where Eddie and I were raised. My brother, Eddie, was born on November 10, 1931. I followed on February 26, 1935. Mother was very involved in Central Christian Church, as well as the YWCA and the Denver Woman's Club. She was a Denver Public Library volunteer, a part of the Great Books program, as well as serving in many other volunteer activities. She was particularly interested in women's and minority rights. I remember her gathering Eddie and I up and going downtown for her YWCA Board meetings. We often swam in the YWCA swimming pool while she was busy. As boys, we were very uncomfortable being in a girl's swimming pool. In the summer, we would play in the pond of Court House Square Park, across the street, while waiting for her. Other days, when she volunteered at the Downtown Public Library, we would go with her and be stashed in the Children's Library. We read and enjoyed the stereopticon viewers and were amazed at the wonders of the world as shown on the thousands of three-dimensional stereopticon slides, just like the ones in the Castle Marne Parlor.

A good friend of hers, Dorothy Roberts, owned The Pooh Corner Book Store. It was located at the alley on 6th Avenue, between Marion and Lafayette, across from the Piggly Wiggly Grocery and Oliver's Meat Market. It was right next door to Bell's Pastry Shop and a block up from the Hiawatha Movie Theater. Mother kept the bookstore's financial records. She was not paid a salary, but she took books in trade. Often Eddie and I would be gathered up and taken to Pooh Corner, while mother worked on the store's financials. Eddie and I would lie on the floor in a corner of the store reading books. In our home, we have three small ladder-back chairs from Pooh Corner that we used to sit in and play under.

It was the summer of 1946, the war was over and father traded in the old Buick for a brand new Plymouth. I was eleven and Eddie was thirteen when mother decided she needed a trip with her kids. Father was very busy at the box company and said he couldn't go with us. Mother understood and went ahead planning a three-week trip to Winnipeg, Canada, for the three of us. I remember the first night we stopped in Hot Springs, South Dakota. I went into the motel office with her. The man behind the counter asked mother if she wanted modern or semi-modern facilities and she said modern. On the way back to the car I asked her what was semi-modern? She said the room had a path to the toilet, outside. We traveled from Mt. Rushmore to Bemidji and to Lake Itasca, where we stepped across the headwaters of the Mississippi River. Then on to Winnipeg.

You remember odd things. There was a racetrack in Winnipeg. One day we looked at a race program and saw that a horse named Dear Helen was running. Eddie and I begged and begged and finally Mother took us to the track where she placed a bet on Dear Helen to win. The horse didn't even place, as I recall.

The trip was a wonderful experience. Looking back, I am now even more amazed by my Mother and the lessons she taught us. We were truly fortunate children to have a mother who gave us her caring love, as well as inspired us with her love of independence, learning, and uncompromised community service.

Mother was a lifelong democrat, while father was a dyed-in-the-wool republican. I can remember how mother would, with tongue in cheek, bait father by telling him not to get so excited about some pressing political issue, as she would cancel out his vote anyway. They exhibited a deep and forgiving love for each other. It was up to us, as their children, to share and make it part of our lives. She died February 22, 1956, of cancer of the lymph nodes, after suffering for several years and three major surgeries. She was 52 years young.

My grandfather, Ferdinand, known to the family as Frank James, was born in Stendal, Germany, July 14, 1868. He came to America with his older brother Franz Otto, who was born on November 17, 1863. They sailed from Bremen in 1883, making their way to Kansas City and finally to Paola, Kansas, where their older brother Christopher, born in 1861, was operating a grocery store.

Otto stayed on in Paola in the bakery business until it burned down. Next, he opened Peiker's Shoe and Clothing Store. The Paola, Miami County newspaper, dated March 25, 1938, featured this headline story: "Fifty four years ago Franz Otto Peiker, honored Paola resident and pioneer merchant, began a most successful career."

Grandfather stayed on in Paola where, we believe, he met and married Anna Katrenia Wilhimina Meitzner in 1891. They eventually moved on to Rosedale, Kansas, where my father, Edwin, was born on January 7, 1899.

The family moved to Denver later that year. In 1904, they moved to Greeley, where grandfather filed for a Homestead Right on 160 acres of dry land prairie east of Eaton, Colorado. My grandfather, father, and two uncles, Albyn and Walter, worked the farm to prove the Homestead Right. Grandmother and my two aunts, Mae and Alice, operated a bakery and restaurant in Ault, where they were able to make enough money to support the family. A third daughter, Louisa, died of scarlet fever on July 3, 1903, at the age of three. She is buried in Denver's Riverside Cemetery.

My uncle, Jake Kohler was born in Lancaster, Pennsylvania, in 1879. He joined the army in 1898. He was sent to Puerto Rico, then to the Philippines, where he saw duty in the Spanish American War. He was discharged in 1903, moving to Denver. Later that year, Jake decided to homestead 160 acres 12 miles east of Eaton, Colorado. He said there was a $24 filing fee for Vets. The next year the Peiker family became his neighbors on an adjoining 160 acre homestead.

In 1913, Jake married my Aunt Mae, the oldest Peiker child. Jake helped the Peikers build their house, barn, and other buildings. Uncle Jake always said that their house would stand as long as he lived. Father bought back the homestead in the 1930s for taxes. For a little while he even thought about moving the farmhouse to his Evergreen property, but never did.

When he died, Eddie and I inherited the farm, which had fallen into serious disrepair. Most all the buildings except the house had fallen down. We leased the property to neighbors for $160 a year to pasture a couple of horses. One day I got a call from the Weld County Sheriff's office. They told me that I had to tear the old farmhouse down. It seemed that kids from Galeton were gathering there late at night and causing trouble. Uncle Jake was still alive (he lived to be 99 years old), and I remembered his prediction that he would live as long as that farmhouse stood. I explained the situation to the sheriff and did we have to knock it down? It turned out he knew Uncle Jake, and he agreed to let it stand, if we would repair the fence and secure the farmhouse as best we could.

Uncle Jake died a few years later, and after attending his funeral in Greeley, we decided to drive out to the farm for old times' sake. Well, you can imagine our shock when we approached the property to see the farmhouse had fallen down. You couldn't make up a story like that.

When grandfather's homestead right was granted, the family sold the property and moved back to Greeley, where grandfather worked for Hackett and Walters, a wholesale bakery. They moved back to Denver in the 1920s, where grandfather worked for Campbell Sells Wholesale Bakery.

My grandfather, Ferdinand (Frank) Peiker was born in 1868 and died in 1948 and my grandmother, Anna Peiker was born in 1873 and died in 1956.

Father seemed to be born under a wandering star, plus he was not happy at home. As a young teenager, he worked in the vanadium mines up Boulder Canyon.

In 1915, he decided to attend the World's Fair, officially known as the Panama-Pacific International Exposition, which opened in San Francisco, California. Ostensibly a celebration of the newly opened Panama Canal, the fair also signaled San Francisco's rebirth following the 1906 earthquake and fire that had reduced the city to a smoldering ruin. Nearly 20 million visitors poured through the gates of the 635-acre Jewel City before they closed on December 15th. On his way west he worked on the 20 Mule Team Borax wagons across Death Valley.

Back home, he lost a bet with some buddies that he couldn't pass the physical to join the army when America entered World War I. He passed, lied about his age, was inducted, and sent to Cuba for training. Because of swimming in the ocean the previous day he had water in his ears and failed the examination for the newly-formed Army Air Corps. He ended up in the Marine Corps, sent to France, where it became known he was underage, and therefore couldn't serve in battle. Instead, he became a motorcycle courier for General Pershing's Headquarters staff.

Although he smoked since he was 14, he always said his later lung cancer and emphysema was due to breathing mustard gas while serving in France.

After the armistice, father moved to Denver where he started a hauling and delivery business. He stabled his horse and wagon in the building at the corner of 18th and Market Street, where the Spaghetti Factory restaurant now operates. He had a delivery contract with the Continental Label Litho & Folding Paper Box Co. In 1922, he went to work for them as the shipping clerk and delivery driver. In 1925, the company moved into Colonel Platt's original paper mill building. By 1933, father was secretary of the company and his older brother Albyn was a salesman. In 1937, father was vice president, Albyn was sales manager, younger brother Walter was a salesman, and Albyn's son Robert was the mail clerk.

In 1939, Clarence Braukman is listed as president and father as V.P. and General Manager. In 1940, the three Peiker brothers bought the company, now listing father as President, Albyn as Secretary and Walter as Sales Manager. Albyn died in 1942, about the time that Continental Paper Products was sold to Central Fibre Products Company of Quincy, Illinois. Their parent company was the Carey Salt Company of Hutchinson, Kansas. It later became part of Packaging Corporation of America, where father was general manager until his retirement on February 1, 1965.

Father imparted to Eddie and I an amazing work ethic and dedication to principle, along with a love of life and sly sense of humor only just buried beneath a rather stiff German bearing. I am certain that I may speak for Eddie that Father's unquestioned love for Mother and us profoundly guided him his entire life.

Reproduction of Peiker Family Crest by nephew,
Greg Peiker. Original found in archives, Wildenman,
Germany.

Diane's Family

Diane's grandmother and grandfather on her mother's side were Bertha Adaline Follmer and Daniel Vincent O'Leary. Her grandmother and grandfather on her father's side were Eva Griffin and Edward Jackson Carpenter III.

Diane's mother, Dorothy O'Leary Carpenter, was born on August 30, 1904, in Fredonia, Kansas. Her family moved to Denver when she was two years old. She graduated from West Denver High School, where she met Les, in 1924. She attended the University of Denver, where she was a member of Kappa Delta Sorority. She was active in the Denver Civic Theater, Denver Symphony Guild, St. Luke's Hospital Guild, and Ascension Episcopal Church Altar Guild. She married Lester G. Carpenter on March 29, 1929. She died December 5, 1962, at the age of 58, of leukemia. Dorothy was a wonderful loving mother who raised four remarkable children. She served her community as Democratic District Captain, much to the dismay of her husband, a

169

republican stalwart. After the death of my mother, Dorothy became an important mother figure to me. Her love and smile warms me still.

Diane's father, Lester Griffin Carpenter, was born in Mancos, Colorado, on February 22, 1906. His family moved to southern Arizona, then to Pueblo, Colorado, and finally settled in Denver in 1915. He was in the first graduating from West Denver High School in 1924, where he was president of his graduating class and star quarterback of the football team. Later he served as president of the West High Alumni Association. He graduated from the University of Denver in 1928, where he was a member of Pi Kappa Alpha fraternity. He received his law degree from Westminster Law School in 1938.

With his business partner, Hollace Jones, they formed Carpenter & Jones, one of Denver's finest real estate firms. They developed many real estate projects in Denver and southwest Colorado during the uranium boom years of the 1950s and 1960s. In the early 1950s they designed and built the award winning Charmony Neighborhood Housing Development in Sterling, Colorado.

He was past president of the Brokers Division the Denver Board of Realtors. He was active in the Masonic Blue Lodge 134 AF&AM, Colorado Conservatory, El Jebel Shrine, the Royal Order of Jesters, Dragoman, Sandblasters, and Legion of Merit. He was also a member of the Denver Athletic Club, and Pinehurst Country Club.

The family grew up at 551 Humboldt Street, next door to both of their grandparents. Les designed and built a home in the Bonnie Brae neighborhood. In 1951, the family moved into their dream house at 825 Cove Way. There were four children in Diane's family. She was the oldest, her brother, Les Jr., known as L.G., was three years younger. The twins, Kenny and Bonnie Susan, came five years later. Diane remembers being told she was responsible for the twins, a duty she took very seriously.

When my young daughter Melissa picked up a Christmas present with a tag that read "From Big Les," she misread it and asked, "Who is Bigles?" In our family, he would thereafter be known and loved as Bigles. I can still hear him saying, "Don't tell me your problems; tell me your successes." He was a good friend, mentor, and father-in-law who I remember with much fondness and love. He died June 3, 1982, at the age of 76.

CHAPTER TWENTY-ONE

Generation II

Melissa's Story

Being in business with my family has been and continues to be, the most rewarding and fulfilling experience I can imagine. It has not always been easy. It has taken great patience, forgiveness and compassion on all sides, to learn to work together. What we have created in this partnership is something beautiful and enriching to both our family and to our guests.

When the family conceived the idea of Castle Marne, Louie and I had been married only a few years. Due to the Savings & Loan Crisis and the subsequent loss of my job, we were forced to rent out our home and move back into my old bedroom in my folk's house. This put extra strain on our new marriage. Dad, having lost his job as well, had extra pressure on his relationship with mom. Louie and my mother were still employed. Luckily they each also had health insurance for us. The four of us had to learn to navigate the roles of adult and child relationships as new partners and equals. I was the child, but now an adult professional. My husband Louie had married into the family. How was he going to establish himself with his strengths?

Dad brought us a lifetime of experience as a salesman and Mom brought the expertise of an educator. Louie brought cutting-edge software computing knowledge and I brought food and lodging experience. Together we each complemented the others, but there was a learning curve. This learning curve meant establishing jobs and responsibilities. Listening to each other and respecting what each brought to the table came with trial and error.

Being tight on money has always been a theme running throughout the nearly thirty years of our partnership. The stress and strain of running this business with such a narrow margin of profit is profound, but at the same time we experience immense job satisfaction. In all four of our professional lives, none of us have loved what we do more than working here at Castle Marne. The feedback and gratitude from our guests about the quality of their stay remind us every day why we do what we do. The sense of satisfaction from a job well done is what we go to bed with every night and what we wake up to every morning.

From the beginning we laughed about "burning the ships." It was a reference to historical explorers who discovered new lands. Many crews became overwhelmed with homesickness or the terror of having to survive in hostile environs. Ship Captains often burned the ships so the crew would not desert or steal the ship to return home. It was, stand together and survive; or die trying. Perhaps in the big scheme of things, starting the Castle Marne was not quite as extreme as those historic endeavors, but to us it was everything in our world. Another trite phrase we've used is "drinking the Kool-Aid." We were committed and there was no going back.

Working with my family means almost every facet of our lives is intertwined with each other. From the financial well-being of the business, to the upkeep and maintenance of the physical building and grounds, to our individual personal physical and emotional health, we are in each other's lives and there is no way around it.

Melissa and Louie in front parlor, 2017.

We're Pregnant!

When Louie and I found out I was pregnant with our first child, we had no idea that our lives would take on a totally new dimension. Three amazing children later, all of our lives are the richer for it. It was June of 1994, when I realized I was finally going to have a baby. Louie and I had been married for 10 years and thought we couldn't get pregnant. We had decided that we were going to find fulfillment in managing the Castle Marne. We had several friends who had no children and knew that our lives would be very meaningful without kids. Now that we were expecting, a whole new life unfolded before us.

Louie and I were living at my folk's house in southeast Denver. Mom and Dad were living at the Castle in what is now our 10th room, the Holland Suite. In the middle of the night on Father's Day, Louie and I got a phone call from Mom telling me that Dad had just had a heart attack. His heart had stopped around 3:00 a.m. We raced across town and dropped Louie off to take care of the Castle, while I rushed to Swedish Hospital. I was six months pregnant. Dad tells the story that he and God had a heart-to-heart talk while he was strapped on a gurney racing to the operating room. Dad informed Him that he was not leaving this earth today to make room for my baby. He was determined to live to meet his first grandchild. Dad loves to tell the story about being wheeled into the operating room, transferred onto the table, looking up at the ceiling, and starting to laugh. There was a picture of a beautiful green lush vista. One of the nurses asked, "What is so funny? You damn near died." He was remembering the scene in the movie *Soylent Green* and said, "If I hear Beethoven's Pastoral Symphony #6, I'm in a whole lot more trouble than I can imagine." Edgar G. Robinson was great in the movie and it was a wonderful book.

Needless to say, Dad survived the heart attack and was at the birth of our first son, Louie James. He helped with the delivery and took pictures, with no film in his camera. In rapid succession, I had two more children; Charles Jozsef and Max Levi. I had three children under five years old and can't imagine how we could have raised them without the help of Mom and Dad. We set up the back bedroom of the Holland Suite with a crib and I would carry a baby monitor with me, so I could be anywhere in the Castle and hear the baby cry.

173

In the early years, we were part of a neighborhood Victorian Holiday Home Tour. There were six historic homes, all within walking distance of each other, decorated for Christmas and open to the public the first Saturday after Thanksgiving. For the tour, I put Louie J. in an antique bassinet and placed him under the Christmas tree in the Parlor. I would talk about the history of the house and its owners and about the work that went into restoring the Castle, while the baby slept peacefully. Only a few guests ever realized that that sleeping child under the tree was a real baby. Now and then, he would wake up and startle the guests. It was fun. We carried it off in grand style with the staff and the whole family in Victorian costumes, including the kids.

As the children grew, we had to come up with safe ways to check guests in, prep and serve breakfast, and run the business. Once the baby was sitting up on his own, we found the perfect solution. We would sit the baby up in the desk drawer, scooch the drawer almost closed, hand the baby the room keys to occupy him and we could take care of business. Guests got a big kick out of seeing the baby help his mom. The baby helped in the kitchen too. We had a saucer instead of a walker, so the baby could jump up and down, twirl around but not actually go anywhere. We would slide the baby in the saucer under the prep counter in the kitchen and work away. We could talk to him, feed him cereal, and sometimes even get a nap out of him.

Over the years we've had regular guests who bounced our kids on their knee and watched the kids grow up. It has been a joy to see the children mature, with a sense of history and recognition of family values ever present. As they were able, they started answering the door, greeting guests, welcoming people to our Castle Marne, and carrying luggage. Later they served breakfast, cleared dishes, and helped around the house. Growing older, they gave tours and told wonderful stories about what it was like to be raised in the Castle.

Louie J. and Charlie driving in the front yard, 1997.

CHAPTER TWENTY-TWO

Generation III
Louis J. ✣ Charlie ✣ Max
Feher-Peiker

Growing Up in a Castle

Louis J.'s Story

The Castle Marne has been around much longer than me. In fact, she is one-hundred & five years older than I am - but for argument's sake she is five years my senior (our family opened our doors for business in 1989). Almost like an older sibling. And she was there for me to support my youth, cultivate my mind, develop my character, and to share her family with me as willingly as she did.

For years, my grandfather (Poppa to those in the know) and I have had the perpetual conversation about how "that beautiful mass of rock & and mortar" has been so inconceivably influential in our lives. Growing up, I always felt that my brothers and I were tremendously spoiled; we not only had wonderfully loving and supportive parents, but we also had the blessing of living and working with at least one pair of grandparents almost every day. Seriously, I saw my grandparents more often than I spent time in the learning halls of my collective K-12 education. Spoiled-rotten in the sweetest way possible.

During my rearing, I was to eat some of the planet's most delicious food in the "four-butt kitchen" of the Marne and the Carriage House gardens. I would test my mettle against heights, bees, grass, hot tubs, snow, and guests with a serious language barrier. One of the more awkward trials growing up was when they would call me over the intercom somewhere on the property and say "Louie J., please come to the front parlor. Louie J., come to the front parlor. Thank you."

CLICK. I would drop whatever I was doing and rush to the front parlor and there would be a parental unit introducing me to a foreign guest who spoke any number of languages. I can specifically recall eight languages with which I was left with to fend for myself for any given amount of time with a guest: Japanese, Korean, Russian, Spanish, French, Pig Latin, Arabic, and even Hungarian. And every time, I turned out just fine. Every international interaction with guests from Mongolia, South Africa, Norway, and Macedonia enriched my life. It opened my eyes to the beauty of the diverse complexity in our world and the intricate and interwoven history that each of our guests has somehow shared with my family and the Marne.

This life of growing up in a castle is one that is tremendously unique and one that can never be replicated. And every step of the way has included my family and the Castle Marne; both having voting power in family meetings, dinner around the table, and planning of holidays. It has early mornings and late nights. More delayed birthdays than not, holidays as well. Saturdays are for swim meets/rehearsal in the morning and serving a back-to-back afternoon tea for twenty-five and a candlelight dinner for six, and that's at thirteen years old. You must be prepared to be the world's most helpful person in every way. You get to come into the office smelling baked goodies and homemade breads. You can choose from three different juices today: Orange juice, Cranberry juice, and the house special Cran-Orange-Berry juice. You

will become very familiar with what the human experience looks like behind closed doors from beautiful to bizarre. You will be delighted by the joy and laughter in the singing from the walls of my home. And you'll definitely want to come back again; I know I always do. Was it tough at times? You bet your Rocky Mountain Oysters it was! Did we get through it? Yes and that was because of the Marne.

Louie James Feher-Peiker, age 23

Charlie's Story

Of course it's contrived to say that something can't be put into words, when someone asks you to say what it was "like" to do this or that. But in all seriousness, I mean that it can't be put into words. Or, at least, it can't be put into few enough words as to make it make sense.

Looking back now, sitting in the attic of the Carriage House, on a cold Halloween Night so much like the ones I spent around the castle as a kid, I'm struck by how many of the memories I can most easily recall are of this place or are in some way tied to it. This stone is the foundation of my upbringing. It is the bedrock of who I am.

I never realized as a child how significant this place was, more than just to my family that is. Of course it was our livelihood and our occupation, but more than that it stood for something that transcends any of the seven of us. What that is entirely, I'm not sure. Maybe it's a way of looking at the world and a way of seeing our relationship with the rest of the human race. I'd like to think that it is.

Everyone is welcome here. We will give everyone who comes through our door the same treatment. They are royalty while they stay at the Castle and maybe that's how it should always be. I wonder what the world would be like if everyone were treated with the same level of dignity, respect, courtesy, and compassion that we try to show our guests. And, so I try to do just that. At first it was my obligation, that I should be pleasant and cordial and compassionate when dealing with guests. However since that was my life growing up here, it became a habit and now it seems I don't know how to do anything else. That, of course, says something about the way of looking at the world.

I don't know if I'm supposed to say this, but it was never about the money. It isn't about the money. It will never be about the money. Nobody in my family has ever seemed to care about money for money's sake, instead we do what we do for the joy of it and because we think, maybe irrationally, that the world would be a better place because of what we try to do. But of course one can only hope.

I don't know if we have been successful, I don't even know if it was worth the effort, but at least we can say that we tried. I can't help but laugh a little, looking around at the accumulated life of three generations and every other life that has passed through this rich,

Charlie Jozsef Feher-Peiker, age 21.

strange old pile of rocks. Everyone who has ever been here and every-thing that has ever happened here has left its mark on this building and on us, the seven of us and everyone else who has been here with us here to see it.

So what did it mean for me? Once again for the cliché, all I can say is that I am who I am because of it. I hope my mom won't get too sappy reading this, but I wouldn't trade it for anything. I don't know who I would be if it hadn't come to pass that out of necessity, frustration and sheer dint of will, that my family came to own and operate the Castle Marne; but, I honestly don't want to know. There is something about this place, and it's not for me to say what, but whatever it is, I'm pretty certain that without it; the world would be sorely lacking.

Max Levi Feher-Peiker, age 19.

Max's Story

As a young child, I didn't grow up like my friends did. Family vacations were short and holidays were delayed until we were able to set a few minutes aside. I was an employee at the age of five, and not fond of these memories, only wishing to be normal and more like my friends. However, what I did find was a different and more independent childhood. Memories that I have held on to most fondly have been meeting guests from around the world, learning new languages, and hearing stories of their travels. Although I might not have experienced such travels myself, I was able to live vicariously through them. I watched many happy couples get married and I learned about hundreds of wonderful traditions.

One of my favorite jobs as a young child at the Castle was to be the concierge. I had established a relationship with many restaurants in Denver, and had made quite the reputation. A the age of six I was close friends with the owner of Il Posto, one of my all-time favorite restaurants. I was sure to recommend them as much as I could. Not only were they one of my favorites, but happened to be right down the street. One afternoon while on the clock I was asked what restaurants

I would recommend that were in their price range, close by, and had wonderful wine and food selections. Mind you, at the age of six I was not at the age for drinking, but I was pals with the sommeliers. They were fascinated with the idea of a six year old being the concierge. I always tried to act more mature for my age. I assured them they would have a wonderful time at Il Posto and that I would be happy to make a reservation for them tonight. I sat down at the desk and dialed the restaurant, letting it ring and ring. They did not pick up their phone. I was determined to get our guest a reservation at the restaurant I had spoken of so highly. I excused myself and asked my parents to visit with them, while I took care of their reservation. I got on my Razor Scooter and rode down the street to the restaurant. Although there was a line out the door, I weaved my way through the crowd, making sure to speak directly to the owner as I didn't want my guests standing in that long line.

When I explained to him that the phone was not being picked up, I was able to arrange for the table with my guests' name on it and have it ready in the next 15 minutes. I rode back up the street and handed my business card to the guests and told them to give it to the waiter. This way he would know who had sent them to the restaurant. Just before they left another couple came downstairs to get dinner reservations and were interested to know more about the Italian restaurant I had just recommended.

By being involved with the family business at such a young age, I was wise beyond my years and had learned to be more comfortable and confident when talking to strangers and adults.

Many Thanks

I want to take this opportunity to express my profound gratitude to all those who helped us in so many and varied ways to make our Castle Marne the very special place we know and love...

To the newspaper and magazine writers who very early on recognized that there was a unique story to be told;

To the bankers and financial advisors who were willing to give us a chance;

To the architects, contractors, trades people and suppliers who advised, explained, and moved us along a sometimes bumpy road to achieve our dream;

To those wonderful advisors and friends in the travel and hospitality industry who told us, showed us, and assured us we could make it happen "our way;"

To those in the public sector who were there when we needed their council and advice to get through the maze of rules and regulations and social strife;

To those who held our hands and led us through the necessary spiritual and physical awareness toward a better understanding of our journey;

To the writers and students of history, novelists, and storytellers who inspired us and contributed their special talents to our endeavors;

To those in our new neighborhood who introduced us and held our hand as we strived to become an integral part of this very special social environment;

And finally, to our friends, both old and new, we want to thank you for your incalculable support and understanding; sometimes questioning, but always there for us.

March 25, 2010, *The Denver Post* Newspaper. Article featuring the whole family.

Eddie and Sue Peiker.

My father, Edwin William Peiker

My mother, Helen Flo Sullivan Peiker

Louie's Parents, Elizabeth and Jozsef Feher

My son Riley and his wife Jessica, Diane and me.

Diane, 2018

Melissa, 2018

"Gratitude is a fruit of great cultivation,
you do not find it among gross people."
Samuel Johnson

I sincerely hope you have had as much fun reading this book as I have had "remembering" and "re-telling" the stories.

A preliminary 1970s renovation prospectus of our inn included the following observation that still rings true today.

> "From time to time, pieces of architecture are built that have such character and fortitude that they survive through the decades of changes in ownership, changes in the surrounding environment and neighborhoods, various uses and misuses, and still emerge intact, with grace and splendor. Such a structure is the house at 1572 Race Street."

I cannot think of a more fitting tribute to our
Castle Marne.

(Above) the Castle in 1887 after construction and (below) how it looks in 2018.

Made in the USA
Columbia, SC
29 August 2018